VANISHING FILIPINO AMERICANS

The Bridge Generation

Peter Jamero

University Press of America,® Inc.
Lanham · Boulder · New York · Toronto · Plymouth, UK

Copyright © 2011 by
University Press of America,® Inc.
4501 Forbes Boulevard
Suite 200
Lanham, Maryland 20706
UPA Acquisitions Department (301) 459-3366

Estover Road
Plymouth PL6 7PY
United Kingdom

All rights reserved

British Library Cataloging in Publication Information Available

Library of Congress Control Number: 2011923174
ISBN: 978-0-7618-5500-2
eISBN: 978-0-7618-5501-9

To my beloved Terri:

Your pride in the Bridge Generation inspired this book. Your love for me made it possible for it to be written.

Contents

Preface	v
Acknowledgments	vii
1. An Invisible Generation	1
2. Growing Up Years	6
3. Youth Clubs	21
4. In America's Workforce	29
5. Civic Participation	41
6. Reunions and Recognitions	49
7. Ordinary Yet Extraordinary	54
Bibliography	108
Index	110
About the Author	114

Preface

According to the U.S. Census of 2000, the number of Filipinos in America increased to 1.8 million, 18 percent of all Asian Americans—the second largest Asian American ethnic group in the country. In California the proportion of Filipinos is even larger at 23 percent of the state's Asian American population.[1] These numbers are a quantum leap from the small band of Filipino immigrant *sakadas* (contract workers) who arrived in 1906 to toil in the sugar plantations of Hawaii. Followed in subsequent years by thousands of other Filipino from the Ilocos and Visayan regions of the Philippines, the *sakadas* would comprise a major portion of the *Manong* Generation.

Today, virtually all of these intrepid souls of the *Manong* Generation are now gone but not forgotten, thanks to the documentation of their experiences in America by researchers and scholars. However, their children—the Bridge Generation—the *Manong* Generation's proudest legacy to the diverse fabric of America, appear to be in danger of being just another distant memory.

At the present time the numbers of the Bridge Generation are rapidly declining. Now in their 60s, 70s, and 80s health issues and death have begun to take their inevitable toll. Funerals and golden wedding anniversaries have replaced marriage celebrations as major social events. Attendance at the old timer Grand Reunions, which previously attracted 600-700 persons, has dropped precipitously in recent years. The dance floors at these old timer reunions, once filled with Bridge Generation couples gyrating to the off-beat and swing, now are only fully occupied when slow music is playing.

This book will chronicle the untold experiences of the Bridge Generation—from their growing up years to their participation in youth clubs, the workforce, and in civic life. As the bridge between the pioneer *Manong* Generation and the several generations of Filipinos in America that followed, the story of this second generation of Filipinos has been neglected. The book is a beginning effort to fill this void.

For members of the Bridge Generation it is hoped the chronicling of their story will not only be a nostalgic trip through time but will also serve to confirm the significant role they played in Filipino American history. For their children and grandchildren and for present-day baby boomer and post-1964 immigrant Filipinos and their children, it is hoped the book will convey the importance that Filipino culture can play in an increasingly multi-cultural America. For other Americans, it is hoped that the story of the Bridge Generation will be seen as yet another example that "only in America" can such a story be told.

Finally, it is the fervent hope of the author that there will be a more far-reaching outcome from the writing of this book—that scholars will undertake a more extensive study of the Bridge Generation's role in Filipino American history and its contributions to America. There can be no greater measure of the book's value and success.

Peter Jamero
Atwater CA
June 2010

Notes

1. U. S. Department of Commerce Bureau of the Census *Twenty-second Census of the United States—2000*. In Linda Espana-Maram *Creating Masculinity in Los Angeles's Little Manila: Working-Class Filipinos and Popular Culture, 1920s-1950s*. (New York: Columbia University Press, 2006), p. 3

Acknowledgments

Foremost among the people to whom I am indebted for writing this book is Terri, my wife of fifty-five wonderful years. She was the first to call my attention to the invisibility of the Bridge Generation in Filipino American history. I thank her for her steadfastness in insisting I was the only one who could do justice to telling the untold story of the Bridge Generation. In so doing, she reprised her role as my inspiration for writing my life story, *Growing Up Brown: Memoirs of a Filipino American*, published in 2006. Terri also performed duties as chief critic, editor, researcher, and proofreader for both books. Sadly, she was not able to see the fruits of her latest work as she passed away on April 2, 2009 at the age of 74.

I am grateful for the artistic talents and technical knowledge of my daughters, Julie Jamero-Hada and Karen Armada, in putting together a manuscript that fulfilled the camera-ready requirements for publication. As busy as they both are in balancing family life with professional life, they did not hesitate in placing top priority on readying the manuscript.

My deep appreciation also goes to Karen and to Cheryl Organo, another of my beautiful daughters, for the necessary but often painstaking task of editing. Karen and Cheryl—thank you for your diligence and patience.

I wish to express my gratitude to my contemporaries—Bridge Generation Filipino Americans—who wholeheartedly have supported my efforts to bring attention to the contributions of our generation to the great country we proudly call the United States of America. I am indebted to the many Bridge Generation individuals who agreed to be interviewed—particularly to those who consented to have their life stories included in the book: Cornelio Pasquil Jr., Fran Alayu Womack, Gabina Hipolito Boiser, Gregory Bautista Bambo, Hildo Pomicpic Jr., Clemente Joseph San Felipe, Jose Valentino Oriarte, Josephine Saito Espineda Paular, Julia Olimpio Arro, Mercedes Arro Concepcion, Nina Dublin Gonzalez, Ray Paular, Rizaline Raymundo, Samuel Catiel Garcia, Samuel Cecil Gonzalez Jr., Virginia Garcia Randall, and Wilma Bucariza Aguinid. Since their interviews, Joe San Felipe and Josie Paular have passed away—an ironic testimonial to the need for this book to be published.

Finally, it is also acknowledged that the above interviews and written materials that have been submitted are primarily based on interviewee recollections. Every effort has been made to corroborate their recollections.

Gratefully,

Peter Jamero

1. An Invisible Generation

Bridge Generation (defined)—"Children born in America by the end of 1945 to at least one Filipino parent who immigrated to the United States during the early 1900s."

Filipino American National Historical Society—
National Conference, 1994[1]

On November 2, 1991 in San Ramon, California, a predominantly Bridge Generation audience of more than 700 listened intently as Filipino American author and historian Fred Cordova asked rhetorically, "Were we hatched from eggs?" His voice boomed as he bemoaned America's failure to acknowledge the existence of second generation Filipino Americans. The eloquent Cordova blamed mainstream media, Filipinos themselves, and academia for the oversight.[2]

Cordova identified a morning daily newspaper, the *Sacramento Union*, as initiating the myth that a second generation of Filipino Americans does not exist when it wrote in 1974:

> America's Filipino community has a singular distinction—one generation is missing.... Middle-aged Filipinos born in this country are few.... Filipino (bachelor) immigrants generally couldn't start families to raise children who in turn would have formed the second generation to build a community. There were few Filipino families for decades. Consequently, a visible Filipino didn't materialize until new waves of Filipino men and women immigrated to the United States after World War II."[3]

The statement has yet to be refuted by the *Sacramento Union* or other mainstream media. It has not been refuted by Filipino American media. To the contrary—in 1994, twenty years after the *Union* article, *Filipinas,* perhaps the most widely read magazine among Filipinos in America, perpetuated the myth when it virtually copied the account of the Sacramento Union by stating, "bachelor workers, therefore, could not start families and produce new generations of Filipino Americans."[4]

The *Sacramento Union* story led most Americans and some Filipinos to buy into the myth. There may be an additional reason that Filipinos have embraced the myth, said Cordova. Some mistakenly equate speaking a native dialect with being Filipino and thus do not view the Bridge Generation—mostly English-only speakers—as Filipino.

Over the years many books, articles, and stories have been published about the manong generation—the intrepid souls from rural Philippine provinces recruited by American agribusiness—that immigrated to the United States by the thousands during the 1920s-30s. While academia turned its attention to the manong generation, continued Cordova, it has completely ignored the experiences and contributions of a significant group of Filipino Americans—the Bridge Generation, the sons and daughters of the pioneer manongs.

Members of the Bridge Generation are now in their 60s, 70s, and 80s. Through the years, many have passed away. Despite going through the same experiences and hardships—such as discrimination in the workplace, education, and in housing—as their Filipino immigrant parents, the Bridge Generation's triumphs and struggles in assimilating into American life has not been documented.

The failure to recognize the contributions of the Bridge Generation has long been decried by Filipino/Asian American observers: "no history, no published literature, no nothing;"[5] "least known and understood;"[6] "not much is known about them."[7] In a related vein, Marie Hong writes in her 1974 anthology *Growing Up Asian American* that prose pieces of Asians coming of age in America is: "... relatively scarce. This is particularly true of Filipino American literature, which, despite its long history, consists mostly of poetry, stories of adulthood, and stories that take place in the Philippines."[8]

The dearth of coming-of-age accounts in Filipino American literature may be coming to an end. In recent years a number of Bridge Generation authors have published memoirs providing sensitive accounts of their personal experiences as second generation Filipino Americans. Patricia Justiniani McReynolds' autobiography *Almost Americans* recounts her years of growing up as a *mestiza* in Los Angeles.[9] Bob Santos' often humorous life story *Hum Bow, Not Hot Dogs*[10] includes rare glimpses into the day to day experiences of living with his boxer father in Seattle's Chinatown. Evangeline Canonizado Buell's *Twenty-five Chickens and a Pig for a Bride* is an emotional and ultimately uplifting account of her life story.[11] This author writes of growing up in a farm labor camp with 100 *manongs* in his autobiography *Growing Up Brown: Memoirs of a Filipino American*.[12]

As significant as these publications may be to the documentation of Filipino American history, however, they only hint at the broader aspects of the Bridge Generation's experience in America. Juanita Tamayo Lott's *Common Destiny: Filipino American Generations* is a positive beginning step in changing direction. In discussing four generations of Filipinos in America, she categorizes the Bridge Generation as the "silent generation"[13] as she concludes:

> My generation, the baby boomers, owes a debt of gratitude to the silent generation. The latter served as a bridge to the pioneer generation before them. The silent generation was clearly aware of the sacrifices of those who went before them. They were dutiful sons and daughters who went on to multiply, not just in terms of becoming parents but through their involvement in various aspects of American society, including education, employment, military service, organized labor, and home ownership. All this was accomplished within extended multiracial family settings, segregated neighborhoods, and in multicultural communities such as Seattle and San Francisco.[14]

In his ground-breaking book *Filipino Americans: Forgotten Asian Americans* Fred Cordova writes:

> It has been a miracle that Filipino Americans—the second-generation in particular—retained a sense of ethnic pride. Too many factors abounded to destroy the Pinoy spirit—lack of role models, parental conflicts, insensitive community leadership, white-ethnocentric teachers, institutional racism, poverty, among them.[15]

Yet, despite these barriers and their negative experiences as brown Americans, the Bridge Generation has indeed survived and persevered. They came of age during the Great Depression, World War II, and the Korean Conflict. They suffered through the tragic assassinations of President John F. Kennedy; presidential candidate, Robert F. Kennedy; and civil rights activist, the Rev. Martin Luther King, Jr. And, they saw the rise of civil rights protections for ethnic and racial minorities, women, disabled persons, and lesbian/gay individuals. Throughout these years, the Bridge Generation was part of the millions of other Americans that helped make the United States the great country it is today. Their story is a story that is yet to be told.

In Filipino American literature, the only study devoting its entire attention to the Bridge Generation is Annalissa Arangcon Herbert's 1996 unpublished thesis, "Growing Up Brown in America: the Filipino-Mango Athletic Club of 1938-1955".[16] Two theories form the framework of her thesis.

- First, is Karl Mannheim's theory of generations in which he postulates that in order to understand different generations one must consider the historical and social context in which the generations exist.[17] In applying the theory to the Bridge Generation, Linda Revilla writes: "Filipino American ethnic identity is assumed to be the product of our historical and cultural backgrounds, and the process of negotiating and constructing a life in the United States."[18]
- The second theory of Herbert's unpublished thesis is from Yen Le Espiritu who theorizes that Bridge Generation Filipino Americans, by struggling between the culture of their parents and that of American society, created a culture that is neither but includes elements of both at

the same time.[19] While her exploratory study focuses only on San Francisco, Herbert concludes that Espiritu's findings can be generalized to other Bridge Generation Filipinos.[20]

Lott's conclusions and Herbert's theoretical framework as they relate to the Bridge Generation is reflected in the following pages and chapters. Discussion will not solely be a scholarly discourse. The net effect of the Bridge Generation's invisibility in Filipino American history has been to essentially ignore the contributions and experiences of a whole generation to the diverse fabric that is America. Therefore, the ensuing discussion will also interweave anecdotal experiences as told by members of the Bridge Generation themselves. Where did they grow up? How did they survive? What were their challenges, their disappointments? What was the degree of their assimilation? What were their achievements?

Hopefully, this telling of their stories will help to begin filling in the void of the Bridge Generation's role in Filipino American history.

Notes

1. This is a modified version of the original definition. I first defined the term "Bridge Generation" for the 1994 National Conference of the Filipino American National Historical Society. However, the rationale for the definition has never been clearly explained. The review of my autobiography *Growing Up Brown: Memoirs of a Filipino American* by Benjamin C. Zulueta in *H-Net Reviews* (December 2007) provides the clarification. Zulueta writes that the phrase "born to at least one Filipino parent" relates to the heavily skewed ratio of immigrant Filipino men to women during the 1920s-30s and the resultant high rate of racially mixed couples that produced the children of the Bridge Generation. "By the end of 1945" was chosen as a cutoff because of the 1946 passage of the Luce-Celler Act which allowed Filipino immigrants to become naturalized citizens. The Luce-Celler Act, together with the War Brides Act of 1945 allowing Filipino American veterans to bring their Filipina spouses to the United States, meant that "Filipino/a childhoods after World War II were substantially different than those before." Finally, Zulueta describes "bridge" as "a cultural bridge, a midway point between the culture of their parents, the culture of the newer immigrants, and that of the United States at mid-century."

2. Fred Cordova, address, The Grand Reunion: Filipino/American Athletic Clubs 1940-1970s, San Ramon, CA, November 2, 1991.

3. Sacramento *Union*, April 18, 1974.

4. Filipinas Magazine, October 1994.

5. Oscar Penaranda, Serafin Syquia, and Sam Tagactac, "An Introduction to Filipino American Literature," in Frank Chin, etal. eds. *Aiiieeee! An Anthology of Asian American Writers* (Boston: Harvard University Press, 1974).

6. Royal F. Morales *Makibaka, the Pilipino American Struggle* (Los Angeles: Mountainview Publishers, 1974). p. 102.

7. Amado Cabezas, Larry H. Shimagawa, and Gary Kawaguichi "New Inquiries Into the Socioeconomic Status of Pilipino Americans in California" *Amerasia Journal* 13:1 (1986-87).

8. Maxine Hong *Growing Up Asian American (*New York: Avon Books, 1993) pp. 15-16.

9. Patricia Justiniani McReynolds *Almost Americans: A Quest For Dignity* (Santa Fe: Red Crane Books, 1997).

10. Bob Santos *Hum Bows, Not Hot Dogs: Memoirs of a Savvy Asian American Activist* (Seattle: International Examiner Press, 2002).

11. Evangeline Canonizado Buell *Twenty-Five Chickens and a Pig for a Bride: Growing Up in a Filipino Immigrant Family* (San Francisco: T'Boli Publishing Co., 2006).

12. Peter Jamero *Growing Up Brown: Memoirs of a Filipino American* (Seattle: University of Washington Press, 2006).

13. Juanita Tamayo Lott *Common Destiny: Filipino American Generations* (Lanham MD: Bowman and Littlefield Publishers Inc., 2006. p. 41. The "silent generation" defined by Lott as "persons born before the Depression through the end of World War II" is essentially the same definition of "Bridge Generation" used in this book.

14. Lott, p. 45.

15. Fred Cordova *Filipinos, Forgotten Asian Americans: A Pictorial Essay, 1763-circa 1963* (Dubuque IA: Kendall/Hunt Publishers, 1983). pp. 164-165.

16. Annalissa Arangcon Herbert *Growing Up Brown in America: The Filipino-Mango Athletic Club of San Francisco 1938-1955* (Unpublished thesis, University of California, Los Angeles, 1996).

17. Karl Mannheim "Sociology of Generations" *Essays on the Sociology of Culture* (Routledge & Paul Press, 1956).

18. Linda A. Revilla "Filipino American Identity: Transcending the Crisis" in Maria P.P. Root ed. *Filipino Americans: Transformation and Identity* (Thousand Oaks CA: Sage Publications, 1997), p. 96.

19. Yen Le Espiritu "The Intersection of Race, Ethnicity and Class: Multiple Identities of Second-generation Filipinos" *Identities* Vol. 1, No. 2-3 (Overseas Publishers Association 1995), pp. 249-273.

20. Herbert, p. 33.

2. Growing Up Years

> *In 1940 only about 54% of the homes in America had complete plumbing—running water, private bath, and flush toilet. Almost a quarter of the homes had no electrical power. . . . Most American homes in 1940 had only 1,000 square feet of living space.*
>
> Tom Brokaw[1]

The Bridge Generation population peaked during the Great Depression and the years immediately before and after World War II. Most lived in the West Coast cities of San Francisco, Stockton, Los Angeles, and Seattle and in the agricultural belts of Central California and Eastern Washington. Significant pockets of Bridge Generation Filipino Americans also could be found in Chicago, the nation's transportation hub. Lacking more definitive population numbers, it has been estimated that 500 second generation Filipino Americans lived in Stockton with another 450 growing up in Seattle in 1946.[2] In addition, 422 Filipinos under the age of 15 were included in Chicago's 1940 Census[3] while in Los Angeles there were 133 Filipino males between the ages of 15 and 24.[4]

Anti-Filipino attitudes by white society, fueled by the real or imagined threats to Great Depression unemployment, forced many Filipinos families to live in predominantly working class and multi-racial enclaves located in the poorest sections in what essentially were segregated city ghettos. They were concentrated in the Western Addition/Fillmore district of San Francisco. In Stockton, it was the area surrounding the intersection of El Dorado and Lafayette Streets and South Stockton. Seattle families largely resided in the Central Area, International District, and points south. In Chicago, where Filipino men married mostly Eastern European women, families clustered around the near North or West Sides of the city.[5]

Single *manongs* resided in hotels and rooming houses, usually in or adjacent to city Chinatowns and Little Tokyo's—King Street in Seattle, Kearney Street in San Francisco, Weller and Temple Streets in Los Angeles, and El Dorado Street in Stockton. There, small Filipino businesses such as restaurants, barbershops, and pool halls were clustered to cater to the *manongs'* everyday needs. These were the businesses that helped support Bridge Generation children and where children often worked to help their parents.

Some of the businesses were engaged in thriving clandestine activities such as gambling or prostitution, which often attracted some of the cities' movers and shakers. Parents kept the clandestine nature of such businesses from their Bridge Generation children. In his unpublished autobiography, Fred Basconcillo writes of his personal hurt after learning that photographs taken of him as a child was with a notorious San Francisco madam who frequented his father's illegal enterprise. The hurt remains to this day even though he now understands that the clandestine business brought more income to the family than could be earned in farm work or in other limited work available to Filipinos at the time.[6]

Most of the year-round *manong* residents living in hotels and rooming houses were employed in service occupations as restaurant workers, bell boys, and domestics. However, once winter came and migratory farm workers moved back to the city for a brief respite, the number of *manongs* ballooned exponentially. The *manongs* provided a rich resource for young Bridge Generation Filipino Americans—besides their parents—to learn more of Filipino culture, values, and belief systems. And since the *manongs* were mostly single, young boys found that they also were a source of learning about some of the seamier sides of life.

For Bridge Generation youth living in city ghettos, the Filipino business section was one of the few places outside of their immediate neighborhood in which they felt welcomed. Other neighborhoods were usually out of bounds. Rudy Delphino describes venturing out of his San Francisco neighborhood as a teenager:

> You would go up to the avenues. They knew that you didn't belong there. You'd go up there and it'd be 'All right kids. Go back where you belong.' Which meant the Fillmore. . . . As a kid, in the late 40s they told you where you belonged.[7]

In Vallejo, Connie Terano remembers going to a theater in her neighborhood where people of color went. However, if she went one block further, white people would stare at her.[8] On a more positive note, another Filipino American would later opine that segregation practices actually contributed to a sense of closeness among young Filipinos as they "stuck together . . . because they had no one else to turn to."[9]

Given agriculture's dependence on the labor of their *manong* elders, a significant number of Bridge Generation Filipino Americans lived in or near farm belt communities in the states of Washington and California. In the 1930s-40s, Wapato and Yakima, Washington and the California communities of Hayward, Salinas, Santa Maria, Sacramento, Vallejo, Livingston, and the tiny delta river towns of Isleton, Walnut Grove, Courtland, and Clarksburg—all boasted significant Filipino populations.

Under these circumstances, growing up for young Filipino Americans meant that their social life was spent with other Filipinos. Recalling the early 1930s in California's rural Central Valley, a *campo boy* recalls:

> the people I knew were like me—Filipino. On those rare occasions when I went to town, I looked in wonder at the strange people who were white, much taller, had long noses, and spoke a strange language. Before I went to school, my world consisted of Filipinos. Everyone else was a foreigner.[10]

In Stockton, downtown businesses routinely posted "No Filipinos Allowed" signs. Filipinos were welcome at "flea house" movie houses such as the Star and Lincoln Theaters in the El Dorado Street neighborhood but rarely to the white neighborhood of Main Street for first-run movies. The Rialto Theater, one of the few Main Street theaters that admitted Filipinos, would always seat them on the segregated right side.[11] Not until after the onset of World War II, when Filipinos suddenly became America's "brave brown brothers", were Filipino teenagers able to enjoy movies on Main Street.

Growing up during the Great Depression was not easy for young Filipinos. Those living in city ghettos often had to step over passed-out derelicts or avoid panhandlers on the streets. Andres "Sonny" Tangalin grew up in Chicago's skid row of McKinley Street where violence, drugs, and drunks were commonplace.[12] Bill Sorro worked as early as eight years of age and recalls selling newspapers in San Francisco on weekends for five cents plus a penny for each paper sold.[13] At age nine, Josephine Loable did laundry at a Delta farm labor camp to supplement her family's income.[14] In Oakland, Evangeline Canonizado and her family "stood in lines for bread, fruits, cereal, and sardines."[15] For many Filipino families, meals were often rice with soy sauce or *mungus* (mungo beans).

If you were a Filipino teen during the Great Depression, chances were that you dropped out of school to help support the family—particularly if you were the eldest son in a large family. As a hundred-pound thirteen-year-old, Toribio "Terry" Rosal stooped over the steamy peat dirt fields of the Stockton Delta to cut asparagus from February to June alongside physically mature *manongs*.[16] After a brief respite, he was off to the Alaska fish canneries where he toiled through the summer months. Then the cycle would begin anew. After serving with the First Filipino Regiment during World War II and the improved opportunities for war veterans that followed, Terry was able to be gainfully employed in less physically demanding work. He never again worked as a migrant laborer.

Those living in rural areas worked in the fields alongside their parents, especially if they happened to grow up in a migrant family. In the 1982 documentary *Dollar a Day, Ten Cents a Dance,* Teresa Romero tearfully describes how she hated constantly moving from the Delta, to the Central Valley, to the deserts of Coachella and back.[17] Another migrant child, Rizaline Raymundo, remembers, "I don't look back on those years as 'those good old days'—not when I now understand the hardships and deprivations."[18] Alex Aguinid, who grew up in

"America's Salad Bowl"—the Salinas Valley—recalls making $2 a month at thirteen years of age in the early 1930s as a janitor at his school sweeping floors and cleaning bathrooms.[19] "During the so-called vacation months" is how Mary Gorre Cantil describes the summers when she and her nine brothers and sisters labored alongside their parents picking tomatoes in the Sacramento Valley as children.[20] "I worked in the strawberry fields (of Santa Maria) from the fourth grade until I graduated from high school," remembers Veronica Roslinda Calibjo.[21] In this connection, the following soliloquy written by Dolores Ladaga Abasolo is poignantly apt:

> In looking back, my family had many hardships, but many happy times, too. Mama was the most wonderful, loving mother, working in the fields from sunrise to sunset to support us. Her beautiful face was marred from the elements and the pesticides used in those days. Her pretty hands and fingers were forever damaged from arthritis. She had to go through what men usually do, toiling in the hot sun or frigid weather.
>
> She always made sure we didn't go to bed hungry and provided for us in as many ways as she could. She always made sure we respected others, went to school, and catechism, and became responsible adults. She loved, protected, and wanted the best for us.
>
> She had to take some of us in the fields when we were little, as we had no baby sitters, or the ones she had (our siblings) were there helping her support our family.
>
> One vivid memory was regarding our baby sister, Lisa, still a toddler. She had to wait in the car or fields while Mama worked; the rest of us were in school or out of the house by then. Towards the end of the day, Baby Lisa trudged down the line to find Mama. When she finally found her, she said, "Mama, when are we going home: I'm heavy" (Meaning she was very tired, waiting in or out of the car by herself).
>
> That was an example of what some farm labor children endured daily, *which still brings tears to my eyes.*[22]

Non-migrant pre-schoolers growing up in the country during the Great Depression had a slightly different experience. Too young to understand the hunger and desolation going on in the rest of the nation, a Central Valley native remembers his early youth as "splendid isolation". His life, similar to Bridge Generation youth in segregated cities, was largely spent with other Filipinos. However, unlike his counterparts who grew up in the city, he did not go hungry in the country where families could grow their own fruits and vegetables, raise their own pigs and chickens, hunt rabbits, catch fish, and pick wild mustard for salad.[23]

In general, Great Depression pre-schoolers were to fare better than older youth born during the decade of the 1920s. By the time these younger Bridge Generation youth reached their teen years in the 1940s, they no longer dropped out of school to help support their families—thanks to a booming World War II economy. More Filipino youth were now found within the halls of local high schools. Moreover, with the assistance of their parents who still bore the scars of being systematically denied educational opportunities, an increasing number of Filipino American youth began to enroll in America's colleges and universities.

However, some Filipino youth were not as fortunate. For them, family obligations, lack of education, and/or workplace discrimination were too much to overcome. Like their *manong* elders, they too followed the crops from Stockton, to Livingston, to El Centro, to Salinas with intermittent stops as *Alaskeros* until the years of back breaking-work took their inevitable toll. Such was the fate of George Plaza, the eldest of five children. Quiet and unassuming, he won grudging respect as a hard worker from experienced *manong* farmworkers from the time he took to the fields at eleven years of age to help support his siblings. Never married, George passed away in 2008 at the age of eighty.

Other youth turned to gangs. Perhaps the best-known Filipino gang was the BG gang that originated in the Northern California community of Gilroy during the early 1940s. The group quickly attracted young Filipinos from Stockton, Russell City in the East Bay, and the small delta river town of Isleton. Organized as a buffer group against the Mexican "pachuco" gangs of the war years, the BG Gang often rode from place to place on their customized motorcycles. They soon became familiar figures in communities with significant Filipino populations. While some of their activities were against the law, only a few gang members spent time behind bars. They enjoyed amiable, if not close, relationships with their Bridge Generation peers, similar to that of the fictional Robin Hood. It was not uncommon, for example, to see BG gang members at social functions and athletic events.[24]

For Bridge Generation girls, their growing up years presented additional challenges. Teenaged girls were regarded as potential mates by lonely *manongs* who—because of anti-miscegenation and the scarcity of Filipinas in America—were denied opportunities to meet marriageable females. Often encouraged by the girls' parents despite what was often a twenty-year age difference, *manongs* pursued girls in the traditional courting practices learned in the Philippines. They brought gifts for the girls and spent most of their visits attempting to impress her parents. Chaperoned by an older relative or by siblings, girls were not permitted to be alone with *manongs*. In 1936 Livingston, Gabina Hipolito was always chaperoned by her family or her godmother when a suitor came to call. At the movies, her father assumed chaperoning as he awkwardly tried to be unobtrusive by sitting in the back row.[25]

Generally, American born *pinays* were not impressed by the lavish attention from *manongs*, for which they had little in common, preferring boys their own age. At the same time, it was not uncommon for Bridge Generation Filipinas, as early as fifteen years of age, to marry *manongs*. For some, it was an opportunity to escape the hardships of poverty and/or a migratory existence. For others, it was for genuine love. Regardless of the girls' initial motivations, many of these relationships resulted in lasting, happy, and successful marriages. In 1946 Jane Romero, then age 16, married Ricardo Loable—21 years her senior. In her biography of Ricardo and after forty years in a successful marriage, Jane, a licensed vocational nurse, writes touchingly and lovingly of her landscape gardener husband as he suffered from the debilitating effects of Alzheimer's disease:

From the town of Janiuay, Iloilo, Philippine Island where he first saw the break of day; to the fields of hard back-breaking labor; to the fields of war where he fought; to his lasting days in the United States where he now exists.These were long journeys for a "Pinoy" to make.Along the way, he suffered hurt and pain but clearly helped pave the way for the next generations of "pinoys". He has reached the age of 83 years old and has struggled all of these days but to the end it will be said that Ricardo, Richard lived all of those lonely, sweating, happy, loving days to find that he did not only survived but that he as a "Pinoy" lived through it all.[26]

Bridge Generation girls did not have the independence and freedom enjoyed by their male counterparts. Filipino parents generally sheltered their daughters from the outside world, raising them to learn the traditional stay-at-home tasks of housework and cooking and preparing them for eventual marriage to a "good provider". In contrast, boys were rarely discouraged from going out with friends, were free to visit girls, and were not as accountable to tell parents of their whereabouts.

Periodic social box dances provided a happy medium for everyone—for sheltered girls, their protective parents, hormonally driven boys, and lonely *manongs*. The candidates earned significant dollars, their parents considered the dances to be a safe social environment for their girls, boys were able to show off the latest steps, and *manongs* had the rare opportunity of dancing with *dalagas* (young women).

Social box dances were fund raising events sponsored by community organizations, usually Filipino fraternal organizations—the Legionnarios Del Trabajo, Caballeros Dimas Alang, or Gran Oriente. Over a period of from three to six months, teen-age girls, properly chaperoned, vied for the title of queen by selling tickets and by going to various community dances to promote their candidacies.

At the candidate social box dances, girls took turns auctioning off a gift-wrapped box—usually an inexpensive item such as a set of handkerchiefs. Supporters began by making small bids for the box that earned the bidder a brief dance with the queen candidate. (Each bid had to be higher than the previous one.) Usually the bidding escalated dramatically, often reaching hundreds of dollars. Small bidders would often pool their money and give it to a more serious bidder, usually a *kababayan* (town mate) thereby increasing the chances of that person to be the winning bidder. The person making the highest bid won the social box and was rewarded with an extended dance with the girl. Proceeds were split 50:50 between the girls and the sponsoring organization.

A candidate for queen could often earn more dollars in one evening than her entire family made in several months. Such was the incentive for Mercedes Arro in 1950 when, after a lengthy campaign, she won out over a host of young *pinays* to become Queen in a contest sponsored by the Legionnarios Del Trabajo.[27]

Bidders were mostly *manongs* since younger Bridge Generation boys usually did not have enough money to make a bid. Therefore, the few free dances—between queen candidate performances—were the only opportunities for Bridge Generation boys to dance, provided they had the right color of ribbon. (The use of different colored ribbons was necessary because of the overwhelming number of single males compared to the few available girls.) Bob Santos recalls their efforts in trying to beat the system in Seattle:

> The guys were charged admission, while the women were allowed in without having to pay. A colored ribbon was pinned on our lapels to show proof that we had paid. A different color was used each week to prevent freeloaders from sneaking in. We tried to outsmart them. We always came as a group to the door where the girls checked in. After we found out the right color of the ribbon for the night, the guys trotted down to the drug store to buy the same color ribbon. It was cheaper.[28]

As may be gathered from the foregoing social box incident, Depression-era Filipino youth were not totally engulfed by the gloom and doom of the times. Like all youth, they could also be fun loving, prone to misbehavior, and become mischievous. In Santa Maria, Veronica Roslinda Calibjo remembers the times that she and her siblings engaged in lengthy strawberry fights by throwing overripe strawberries at one another in the fields when their parents were not there to supervise.[29] In Livingston, the Jamero brothers secretly read comic books in an adjoining bamboo grove when they should have been tending to irrigating the grape vineyard.[30]

Sometimes youth could get into trouble when they were only trying to help. Ernie Cabreana tells of an incident at a Sunday *sabong* held at an isolated site among the eucalyptus trees near the tiny Central Coast community of Nipomo, California. Asked to fetch water in town, he recalls:

> Being the wild one I was in those days, I showed off by dumping the clutch (of my hot rod) and pealed out of the Arena with loud pipes blaring. When we returned after filling the jugs, we had a reception waiting for us. The head sabongero (handler of fighting roosters) and chicken fighters were very angry with me and looked like they were ready to kill me. You ever see a Pinoy pissed off?
>
> Reason was . . . I had scared the chickens when I pealed out of the Arena and they panicked and flew off into the woods. The head sabongero gave me a tongue-lashing. He called me, among other things, a panggulo (troublemaker) and to never drive my jalopy to the sabong again.[31]

By the 1940s, a critical mass of second generation Filipinos was in place, clearly visible within minority city ghettos and in isolated rural pockets. As noted by Herbert[32] and Lott[33] achieving a critical mass—by fostering group identity—is a prerequisite to the development of ethnic identity. Group identity was significant to the Bridge Generation—struggling as they were with the common dilemma of reconciling the inconsistencies of traditional Filipino culture with the reality of contemporary American life.

Whether they grew up in the city or country, young Filipino Americans began to develop similar views of the world. They regarded the regionalism beliefs of their parents, for example, as contrary to the quest for their own ethnic identity within diverse America. The Philippine region or province from which their friends' family happened to originate was not relevant. Young Filipinos believed that it was more desirable to be inclusive in their choice of Filipino friends. They judged people as individuals, not by where they came from.

The Bridge Generation's preference for inclusiveness was so strong, unquestioned acceptance of non-Filipinos into their group was commonplace. In San Francisco, Otto Niduaza, a light-skinned youth of European/South American parentage, was unanimously elected as one of the first members of the Mango-Filipino Athletic Club. Chinese American Chris Gin was a long-time compatriot of Bridge Generation Filipinos in Salinas. Similarly, Bob Murray, an African American who "hung out" with young Filipinos in Seattle, was considered Filipino by his Bridge Generation friends and was accordingly introduced to outsiders as such.[34] Not surprisingly, all three of these "non-Filipino Filipinos" grew up to marry *pinays* (Filipinas).

The Bridge Generation similarly rejected the Philippines traditional preference for so-called "pure Filipinos" rather than those of mixed ethnicity. As bachelors, their fathers had few opportunities to meet and marry Filipinas since the ratio of Filipino men to women was 14:1.[35] Consequently, many of their unions were to women of other ethnic groups.

The *mestizo* (mixed parentage) children resulting from these unions regarded themselves as Filipino and were regarded as such by their contemporaries. *Mestizos* in California were largely Filipino-Mexican due to the commonality of their Roman Catholic faith, Spanish influenced culture, and brown skin. While never denying his Mexican heritage, the life choices that Dick Supat of Sacramento made in marrying a Filipina and socializing with other Filipino Americans are clear indicators that he regarded himself primarily as Filipino. Isleton's John Maglinte, whose parents met and married in Hawaii where plantation life resulted in many Filipino/Japanese unions, made similar life choices.

Unlike California's experience, the unqualified acceptance of mixed-race Filipinos by their Bridge Generation counterparts was not the pattern in Chicago. There, children tended to identify primarily with their white mothers rather than with their Filipino fathers. Barbara Posadas[36] cites two contributing factors, not present in California. First, most Filipino fathers worked as railway porters and cooks, which took them away from home for lengthy periods. Second, Chicago lacked a critical mass of youth that resided in relatively close proximity to one another.

In Seattle, the ethnic identity chosen by Indo-Pinos—the children of marriages between Filipino men and Native American women—went in various directions. While some Indo-Pinos primarily identified with Filipino culture, others considered themselves mainly Native American. All interrelated comfortably between the two ethnic groups. Bernie (nee Reyes) Whitebear, who led the successful takeover of Fort Lawton during the early 1970s on behalf of "Indians of All Nations," was often a regular at informal social gatherings of Bridge Generation Filipino Americans. Bob Santos, whose mother was a quarter Canadian Indian, was in great demand as a speaker at Native American events.

The Bridge Generation may not have known it at the time, but their ready acceptance of mixed Filipinos, particularly in California, was ahead of its time by fifty years. In 1997, in writing about the conflicts that have nevertheless continued within the Filipino community through the ensuing years, Maria Root concludes:

> As self-identified mixed heritage people, to empower ourselves, we must refuse to account for ourselves in fractions—one-half Filipino, one-half something else—which is an act of colonizing identity; we must refuse to be gatekeepers of racial authenticity; we must refuse to participate in divisions originating in class, phenotype, education, dialect, and nativity.... We must respect the diversity in our community rather than strive to eliminate or ignore it.[37]

During the '40s, mixed children were believed to account for more than half of second generation Filipinos.[38] Today, *mestizos* continue to comprise a significant proportion of the Bridge Generation population.

Whether their mothers were Mexican, Native American, Asian, black, or white, most Bridge Generation *mestizo* children were raised in the Filipino culture of their *manong* generation fathers. Their mothers had long been accepted into the family and social networks of their Filipino husbands. They learned to cook Filipino food. A Canadian of European ancestry, Emma Galanida, was such an excellent cook that her out-of-town nephews regularly came by her Sunol, California home in 1952 to savor her chicken and pork *adobo*, a stew made with vinegar and spices. Some mothers learned to fluently speak a Filipino dialect. Juanita Hernandez Pomicpic Nambatac of Delhi California, born and raised in Mexico, regularly engaged in animated patter in the Cebuano dialect with her *manong* and *manang* contemporaries—inevitably eliciting incredulous comments from her Filipino friends on how well she spoke the dialect.

The quest to balance traditional Filipino values of their parents with American culture resulted in other interesting contrasts. While their fathers spoke the native dialect, the Bridge Generation usually responded in English. Felix Duag of San Francisco recalls: "I could understand Tagalog and Visayan. Never spoke it because my parents wanted me to speak English ... they spoke to you in the dialect but they didn't expect you to answer."[39]

The Bridge Generation's use of English was also an affirmation of their status as American- born Filipinos. Their preference for English did not preclude identifying as Filipino. Contrary to popular belief, research has indicated that speaking a native language is not necessary in ethnic identity formation.[40]

Not only was English the Bridge Generation's language of choice; they liked jazz, relished hotdogs and hamburgers, and played basketball and baseball with a passion. They considered themselves Americans—but with a difference. They saw themselves as brown Filipino Americans with their own identity and culture. Young Filipinos spoke in G language inspired by the Pig Latin that was in vogue in America during the '40s. They referred to themselves as "Flips" but considered the term a racial slur when used by others. They created the offbeat to dance to bebop jazz music and were adept in dancing the Rumba and Cha-cha.

Unlike their parents, Bridge Generation Filipinos had little interest in events in the Philippines. They did not share the Filipino passion for cockfighting although there were a few, such as Sonny Pomicpic of Livingston, Felix Bunac of Santa Maria, and Tim Maghoney of Isleton, who dabbled as neophyte *sabon-*

geros. Bridge Generation Filipinos also resented the colonial mentality of their parents' generation, especially when they robotically deferred to the supposed righteousness and superiority of white persons.

> At parties, we did not automatically seat white persons at the best tables just because they were white. We did not assume that white people were superior or blindly accept their views. We did not believe that only whites were American. After all, we were Americans too.[41]

Most second generation Filipinos resisted their parents' efforts to join fraternal organizations such as the Legionnarios Del Trabajo, Gran Oriente, and the Cabelleros Dimas Alang. During the 1960s, Stockton's Daguhoy Lodge of the Legionnarrios Del Trabajo established a Junior Lodge. It was hoped that early participation of youth would provide a natural progression to the lodge. Its impact was only short term. While the effort attracted many young Filipinos to the Junior Lodge at the outset, most had dropped out of the organization by the end of the decade.

At the same time, young Filipinos generally followed Filipino customs and cultural norms. They ate steamed rice with their meals, savored traditional Filipino dishes like *adobo*, and always referred to their elders by respectful names such as *Manong* or *Manang, Lolo or Lola* (grandfather or grandmother), and "Uncle" or "Auntie"—never by their first names. In addition, like their elders who had a penchant to use names that described physical characteristics, Bridge Generation Filipinos also generated a variety of inspired nicknames such as Big Boy, Flip, Toscani, and Pee Wee. Perhaps the most colorful and imaginative of nicknames were those that young people answered to on Stockton's busy El Dorado Street—Sleepy, Poaches, Ham, Corny, Big Kanak, Little Kanak, Paddles, and Toad.[42]

As noted previously by Linda Revilla, Filipino American ethnic identity is determined within the historical and social context in which the Bridge Generation existed. In the decades of the '40s and '50s, most minority youth were not referred to as Americans, even though they were born in the United States. Bridge Generation members were called Filipino—not American, not even Filipino American. This phenomenon is discussed by Joe San Felipe whose father was of Filipino and Spanish parentage and mother was English, Scotch, and Irish:

> The term of hyphenated American didn't exist. If you were of mixed or if you were of non-Caucasian ancestry....you were identified as having the nationality of your parents. If you had Chinese ancestry, you were Chinese. There were no Chinese Americans. . . . If you were Mexican American you were Mexican. If you were Filipino American, you were Filipino. And the Caucasian kids, no matter what their European ancestry, European background were all the American kids. And so you felt . . . a lack of identity with the community at large.[43]

Not all young Filipino Americans were comfortable with being identified as Filipino. "In 1940s California, Hawaiian was acceptable." writes Patricia Justiniani McReynolds as she recalled her youth in Los Angeles.[44] Another Filipino growing up in Hawaii was similarly conflicted: "Filipino culture . . . I saw as the culture of my parents and their friends. While I participated in Filipino activities, I did so mechanically mainly to please my parents."[45]

As with other ethnic minorities, Bridge Generation Filipino Americans also encountered discrimination. In the California Delta, some schools were segregated; Eddie Romero went to grade school in Isleton where his classmates were exclusively Filipinos, Japanese, and Chinese children—white children went to their own school.[46] American-born Liz Megino of Oakland recalled being told to go back to the country she came from.[47] As she trained for the 1948 Summer Olympics, soon-to-be diving champion, Vicky Manalo Draves, could not practice in the segregated pools in her home town of San Francisco.[48]

Felix Duag remembers that in San Francisco: " . . . you couldn't go to the beach, to the swimming pools. Do you know the Sutro Pools? You couldn't get in there if you were Filipino. You couldn't go into the Fairmont Hotel and go swimming 'cuz you were Filipino."[49]

Growing up in the north bay city of Vallejo, Connie Terano experienced discrimination at a very young age.

> I remembered there was a See's candy store in the same block. So I went there to buy a piece of candy. The lady in the store asked if I had any money. When I showed her my money and pointed to the piece of chocolate candy I wanted, I remember her taking double pieces of paper so she wouldn't touch my hands. Being the child that I was, I purposely dropped the money on the floor. She had to come around the corner to pick it up. I was about eight at the time.[50]

Education was highly valued in Filipino families and served as a major force in helping to assimilate the Bridge Generation into American society. Young Filipinos generally did well in the classroom and got along with their classmates. Socially, however, it was not unusual for them to be excluded. A Bridge Generation Filipino, popular among his classmates and president of his high school class, was the only one not invited to a party of class officers in San Francisco. Ironically, the party was in a Jewish home.[51]

After being turned down repeatedly by white girls, another popular high school class president came to the realization the only way he could go to the Junior Prom was if his date was of an ethnic minority. Devastated, he chose not to attend the event rather than told whom he could bring.[52]

Some Bridge Generation Filipinos went to high schools with few other Filipinos or minorities, if any. Consequently, social activities could be severely limited. While the youth club movement, particularly in California, helped to fill the void, Filipino American students were on their own when it came to having a social life at school. Nina Gonzalez' high school experience was typical of how some students handled their situations. "During my high school years, I had two sets of friends—white friends, usually Portuguese Catholics in school and Filipino kids when I was outside," says Nina. Gravitating toward white friends who were Portuguese Catholics is significant. Nina explains, "My mother taught me to stay with my own kind, but since it was not always possible in school, I socialized with those who I had something in common."[53]

Dating white girls was not acceptable in the growing up years of Bridge Generation Filipinos. In San Francisco, Joe San Felipe, of Filipino-Caucasian ancestry, recounts his experience after taking a white girl to Sunday Mass:

> The next day at school Jean comes up to me and says, "I can't see you anymore . . . my father doesn't think it's right. He didn't know you were Filipino." I wondered to myself what he thought I was. . . . You can't date the Caucasian girls from the nicer families. You can't go to nice restaurants. You can't go to certain social affairs.[54]

World War II and its aftermath was an important turning point for the Bridge Generation. Young Filipinos did not hesitate to enlist in the armed forces. It was an opportunity to demonstrate their strong sense of patriotism and identification as Americans. Many served in the U.S. Army's First and Second Filipino Regiments of 7,000 men, overwhelmingly consisting of *manongs* born in the Philippines. The regiments would see action in the Philippines—first, as General Douglas MacArthur's secret advance body, and then, as part of the force that liberated the country from the Japanese. Their exploits were featured in a 2001 documentary, *An Untold Triumph: America's Filipino Soldiers*, spearheaded by Domingo Los Banos of Hawaii, a First Filipino Regiment veteran and Bridge Generation Filipino.[55]

During World War II, America called them "brave brown brothers" for their service. Upon their return home, they were hailed as heroes. Shortly thereafter, however, Bridge Generation war veterans would again encounter discrimination. Decorated veteran Antonio "Dixon" Campos—one of the first members of the Filipino Mango Athletic Club of San Francisco and highly respected among young Filipinos—and his new bride, Elisa, were barred from purchasing a home simply because of the color of their skin.[56]

Young returning veterans of the Korean War similarly experienced housing discrimination. In 1953 two Bridge Generations students, one of whom received a Silver Star and Purple Heart for bravery in battle, were college students at San Jose State when they, along with three other Bridge Generation students, were evicted without notice. Legislation prohibiting housing discrimination was yet to be enacted. With no other recourse, the two veterans consequently wrote identical letters to San Jose State and the city's two daily newspapers protesting their treatment. One of the students recalls his disappointment:

> I consider the community response to have been ineffective. There was nothing in the way of lasting change. No one in the neighborhood came forward in support or to join in opposition. No official from San Jose State offered assistance. Civil rights organizations . . . were conspicuous by their absence. Most frustrating was the absence of support from San Jose's well-established Filipino community. . . . I soon faced the sad and sober fact that this incident was of significance only to us.[57]

The foregoing examination of the Bridge Generation's collective growing up experiences in America reflects Mannheim's theory discussed in the first chapter—that one must consider the historical and social context in which the generation exists. Espiritu's theoretical premise—that second generation culture is neither the culture of their parents nor of American society, but includes elements of both—appears to be similarly reflected.

This chapter has focused on the growing up years of second generation Filipino Americans which, in turn, led to the development of a unique sub-culture—that of the Bridge Generation. The sub-culture's rapid spread from California through the West Coast was aided by the Bridge Generation's network of friends and relatives—built through the years by the migratory life of their "uncles", the strong family ties maintained by their parents, and their own summer experiences of working in the agricultural fields in the Delta and Central Valley or in the canneries of Alaska. Thus, G language soon was spoken in small towns like Isleton and Livingston as well as in the big cities of Los Angeles and San Francisco. In addition, because young Filipinos became part of the *Alaskero* workforce, the offbeat soon was danced in the ballrooms of Seattle, gateway city to Alaska.

As significant as these factors may have been, however, it was the serendipitous rise of Filipino youth clubs in California that cemented the emerging sub-culture into the hearts and minds of Bridge Generation Filipino Americans.

Notes

1. Tom Brokaw *The Greatest Generation* (New York: Random House 1998) p. 205.

2. Fred Cordova *Filipinos: Forgotten Asian Americans, A Pictorial Essay/1763-circa 1963* (Dubuque, IA: Kendall/Hunt Publishing 1983) pp. 159-160.

3. Barbara Posadas "Mestiza Girlhood: Interracial Families in Chicago's Filipino American Community" in *Making Waves: an Anthology of Writings by and about Asian American Women* (Boston: Beacon Press, 1989), p. 274. Note: The 1940 Census would be the last census in which Bridge Generation children can be assumed (those born before 1946).

4. Linda Espana-Maram *Creating Masculinity in Los Angeles's Little Manila: Working-Class Filipinos and Popular Culture, 1920s-1950s.* (New York: Columbia University Press, 2006) p. 140. (See note in 2 above).

5. Posadas, p. 177.

6. Juanita Tamayo Lott *Common Destiny: Filipino American Generations* (Lanham, MD: Bowman & Littlefield Publishers, Inc. 2006). pp. 42-44.

7. Rudy Delphino interview in Annalissa Arangcon Herbert *Growing Up in America: The Filipino-Mango Athletic Club of San Francisco 1938-1955* (unpublished thesis, UCLA, 1996). p. 5.

8. Yen Le Espiritu *Filipino American Lives* (Philadelphia: Temple Univ. Press, 1995) p. 70.

9. Fred Basconcillo interview in Herbert. p. 67.

10. Peter Jamero *Growing Up Brown: Memoirs of a Filipino American* (Seattle: University of Washington Press, 2006). pp. 18-19.

11. Filipino Oral History Project *Voices: A Filipino American Oral History* (Stockton: 1984).

12. Andres "Sonny" Tangalin interview June 22, 2008.
13. Bill Sorro "A Pickle for the Sun" in Helen Toribio ed. *Seven Card Stud with Seven Manangs Wild: An Anthology of Filipino American Writings* (San Francisco: T'Boli Publishing, 2002). p. 168.
14. Ronald Takaki *Strangers From a Different Shore: A History of Asian Americans* (New York: Penguin Books, 1989). p. 343.
15. Evangeline Canonizado Buell *Twenty-Five Chickens and a Pig for a Bride: Growing Up in a Filipino Immigrant Family* (San Francisco: T'Boli Publishing Co., 2006). p. 8.
16. Cordova, p. 159.
17. *Dollar A Day, Ten Cents A Dance: A historic Portrait of Filipino Farm Workers in America* (Impact Productions, 1984) video cassette.
18. Rizaline R. Raymundo *Tomorrow's Memories: A Diary, 1924-1928* (Honolulu: University of Hawaii Press, 2003), p.xvii.
19. Alex Aguinid "The Laborer" *Filipino Journal* Vol. 4, No. 4, 1994-1996, p. 3.
20. Mary Gorre Cantil letter, September 3, 2008.
21. Veronica Roslinda Calibjo *Biography* in *Stories, Legends, and Memories* (Santa Maria: Filipino American National Historical Society, Central Coast Chapter 2008). p. 55.
22. Dolores Ladaga Abasolo manuscript, November 5, 2008.
23. Jamero, p. 16.
24. Jimmy Bucol interview, July 26, 2008.
25. Gabina Boiser interview, April 8, 2008.
26. Josephine Loable, Epilogue to "Pinoy" (unpublished biography of Richard Palma Loable, 1991).
27. Mercedes Arro Concepcion interview, June 10, 2008.
28. Bob Santos *Hum Bows, Not Hot Dogs: Memoirs of a Savvy Asian American Activist* (Seattle: International Examiner Press, 2002), p. 32.
29. Calibjo, p. 55.
30. George Jamero interview, April 8, 2008.
31. Ernie Cabreana *Hot Rodding to the Sabong* in *Stories, Legends, and Memories* (Santa Maria: Filipino American National Historical Society, Central Coast Chapter 2008), p. 33.
32. Herbert, pp. 19, 69.
33. Lott, p. 278.
34. Santos, p. 34.
35. Juanita Tamayo Lott "Demographic Changes Transforming the Filipino American Community" in Maria P.P. Root ed. *Filipino Americans: Transformation and Identity* (Thousand Oaks, CA: Sage Publications, 1997), p. 13.
36. Posadas, pp. 273-282.
37. Maria P.P. Root "Contemporary Mixed-Heritage Filipino Americans: Fighting Colonized Identities" in Maria P.P. Root ed. *Filipino Americans: Transformation and Identity* (Thousand Oaks, CA: Sage Publications, 1997), p. 89.
38. Cordova, p.164.
39. Felix Duag interview in Herbert, p. 43.
40. Revilla, p. 105. Also refer to Lombos-Wlazlinski *Social and Psycholotgical Determinants of Language Shift: The Case of the Filipino Community in the City of Virginia Beach VA* (Paper presented at the International Philippine Studies Conference, Honolulu, April 1996).
41. Jamero, p. 77.
42. *Liwanag* (Liwanag Publishing, Inc., 1975). p. 210.

43. Joe San Felipe interview in Herbert, p. 61.

44. Patricia Justiniani McReynolds *Almost Americans: A Quest For Dignity* (Santa Fe: Red Crane Books, 1997). p. 252.

45. L. Andaya "From American-Filipino to Filipino-American" in J. Okamura & R. Labrador Eds. *Pagiriwang 1996: Legacy and Vision of Hawaii's Filipino Americans* (Honolulu: University of Hawaii, Student Equity, Excellence, and Diversity; Center for Southeast Asian Studies, 1996), p. 6.

46. Ed Romero interview, San Jose, CA, August 11, 2008.

47. Takaki, p.343.

48. In order to use the pool Vicki Manalo had to "pass"; she used her mother's maiden of Taylor instead of Manalo.

49. Felix Duag interview in Herbert, p. 53.

50. Espiritu, p. 74.

51. Felix Duag interview in Herbert, p. 52.

52. Jamero, p. 75.

53. Nina Gonzalez interview, April 8, 2008.

54. Joe San Felipe interview, in Herbert, p. 51.

55. *An Untold Triumph: America's Filipino Soldiers* (documentary, Noel M. Izon, Executive Producer, 2001) video cassette.

56. Ibid.

57. Jamero, p. 102.

3. Youth Clubs

One can conclude that participation in an ethnic based club can have a positive effect on the self esteem of the participants.

Annalissa Arangcon Herbert[1]

The youth club movement began in 1939 when the Filipino Mango Athletic Club of San Francisco was established by five young Filipino Americans—Ernie Bala, Julian Calagos, Ben Marcelo, Cris Punzal, and Cepy Villanueva. The following year, they were joined by Antonio "Dixon" Campos, Ed Campos, Vince Cobalis, Henry Cubillo, Felix Duag, Ernie Encelan, Larry Sabrido, Clemente "Joe" San Felipe, Frank "Babe" Samson, and Ted Tabelleja—comprising the basic team that would dominate Filipino American basketball for the next ten years. Perhaps just as important, these young players were the core group that would go on to play significant roles in the emerging youth club movement in California.

The original reason for establishing the Filipino Mango Athletic Club was to participate in city-wide basketball tournaments. Its stated goal read, "To interest and develop the Filipino youth of our community in a better understanding of friendship and good citizenship ... through sports and social activities."[2] With the addition of ten more members, the Mangos took on a more far reaching objective. It now was able to play other nearby Filipino basketball teams on a home-and-home basis.

From the outset the Mangos set a high standard for athletic and organizational excellence. On the court, it won virtually all its games. Organizationally, it was selective in the members it chose to include in the club, requiring interested youth to go through a rigorous application process for membership. The following application letter dated April 19, 1950 from James Mullen is instructive:

> I have been watching the progress of the Mangos as a club and I feel quite envious of its members because of their social and athletic opportunities. . . . I am writing this letter of introduction from information I have gathered from its members. I am of Filipino descent and I am seventeen years old. I am not very good as an athlete but I am willing to try. I hope I can make the grade for the membership of the Mangos and I will try to keep up its fine reputation.[3]

Mullen, a mestizo Filipino, was accepted as a full-fledged Mango.

When it first began organizing in 1939, the Mangos sought sponsorship from the Filipino Community Inc. only to be told, "Go out and prove yourselves and then we will consider sponsorship."[4] Disappointed but undaunted and realizing they would have to go it alone, the Mangos put on a number of successful fund raisers enabling them to purchase uniforms and equipment and to pay entry fees for the city league and various tournaments. On the athletic field, the Mangos were dominant as they usually disposed of other Filipino Bay Area teams and strongly competed in San Francisco city leagues.

Most importantly, the Mangos found equal success in organizing and managing the organization. Their fund raising events were immensely successful. Dances were well attended as the club was able to attract many musicians in the bay area, such as future jazz great Cal Tjader, to play for them.[5] Their finances were always accountable. There were so many requests from youth to join the Mangos that it almost became unmanageable to accommodate them all. The organization that started with five youth in 1939 would soar to over a hundred Bridge Generation young persons by the end of the '40s.[6]

After the Mangos achieved a solid record of success, the Filipino Community Inc. finally offered to sponsor the club. But now, flushed by their ability to support themselves and maintain success on the basketball court, it was the Mangos who rejected the Filipino Community Inc. The Mangos would never seek sponsorship again.

World War II interrupted the Mangos' development as most members went into the armed services or into the merchant marine. Many Mango club members served with the U.S. Army's First and Second Filipino Regiments that won fame as advance scouts that secretly prepared the way for General Douglas MacArthur's triumphant return to the Philippines and later helped secure the country in mopping up operations.

Ironically, the war also made it possible to greatly expand the youth club movement. While in uniform, Mango club members met other Bridge Generation Filipinos from other areas and shared their club experiences. With the end of hostilities in 1945, a number of these young war veterans returned home and organized youth clubs in their own communities.

The founding of the Livingston (CA) Fil-American Youth Club in 1947 was a typical example. Army veteran Frank Padin, a native of the Hawaiian island of Maui, came to Livingston to live with his uncle, Procesio "Sesong" Navarres, to attend nearby Modesto Junior College on a baseball scholarship. Uncle Sesong had long been concerned about local Filipino youth in the small Central Valley community. Every Sunday, he would see several dozen youth who had accompanied their parents to the weekly sabong (chicken fights) without anything to do. He worried that, left to their own devices, the young people invariably would get into trouble.

Frank, older than most of the Livingston area's Filipino youth, provided the perfect answer for his uncle. He organized the boys into several basketball teams—regardless of experience or skill level. The boys were impressed with the older Filipino's stardom as a college centerfielder, with his exotic life in far-off Hawaii, and with Frank's patriotic service during WWII. They were especially impressed that he encouraged all boys to participate in sports—regardless of their skill level—and immediately took to Frank as the role model and leader they needed. His old Mango army buddies in the Bay Area provided him with guidance in organizing a youth club. And because Frank believed in a coed approach, he also insisted on club membership for girls.

With the strong support of Uncle Sesong and the able assistance of local youth Trongkilino "Chunky" Dacuyan and Herb Jamero, the Livingston Filipino American Youth Club "Dragons" became a reality in 1948. It was also fortuitous that ex-San Francisco Mangos, Julian Calegos and Ted Tabellija, would soon move into the area. Because of the club, youth now were able to take trips to the snow, to the ocean, to the city, and participate in other wholesome activities. For virtually all of these relatively isolated young country kids, these were first time experiences. During the next twenty years, the Livingston Dragons would be a consistent contender in athletic tournaments and provide young boys and girls with opportunities to hone their self-image and ethnic identity as Bridge Generation Filipino Americans. In the 2008 anthology published by the Central Valley Chapter of FANHS (Filipino American National Historical Society), Herb Jamero reflects:

> The tournament days are treasured memories. Being young, we could play all day and dance until 1:00 a.m., go out for early morning food at a restaurant then drive two hours to get home. The Livingston Dragons experience enabled each of us to come to better terms and understanding in our evolving identity as Filipino Americans. This experience developed a special camaraderie with our own club members and those from other communities as well.[7]

Frank Padin was not the only youth club organizer during the 1940s. In the North Bay, Pete Serrano and George Oriarte founded the Vallejo Filipino Youth Recreation Association while Albert "Corky" Bueno and Leo Escalante established the San Jose Agenda in the South Bay. In heavily populated Stockton, the Filipino Catholic Youth Society Padres was established by Pete Galvez, the Stockton Fils was founded by Leo Carido, and Al Atentico and Abe Valderama organized the Filipino Youth Association. Virginia Garcia had the honor of being the only female among the initial youth club organizers. Along with Sonny Majarucon, she prevailed upon the Roman Catholic Sacred Heart Parish to sponsor the Salinas Filipino Youth Council in order to serve the burgeoning Bridge Generation population of America's Salad Bowl.[8]

These clubs were followed in short order by the following clubs representing virtually every Bay Area/Central Valley community populated by Filipinos: Vallejo Val-Phi, San Francisco Filipino Youth League, Stockton Trinity-Presbyterian, Oakland Mabuhay, Stockton United Filipino Youth, Sacramento Filipino American Youth Club Royals, San Francisco Bay Area Bards, Stockton Eagles, Isleton Hawks, Delta Knights, Oakland Bohol Circle, Sacramento Carabaos, Stockton Centaurs, Bay Area Intrepids, Vallejo FilDons, Fremont Bolos, Antioch Rascals, San Jose Solidarians, San Francisco Tamaraws, Mt. View Eagles, Fremont Hi Fi, and the Pittsburg Filipino Youth Club Islanders.

Occasionally, other California teams from Los Angeles, San Diego, Fresno, Delano, Lodi, Walnut Grove, and Santa Maria would compete. In 1950, Seattle, Washington was represented by a team—the Cavaliers—that drove all night to participate in a Stockton basketball tournament. Too tired to play their best, the team did not fare well but, to this day, still talk about the great time they had meeting other Bridge Generation youth.[9]

A few youth clubs—the Stockton Filipino Catholic Youth Society Padres, Salinas Filipino Youth Council, and the Stockton Trinity-Presbyterian—enjoyed community sponsors. Most clubs, however, were self-supporting and self-sufficient. They learned to raise money, pay for their expenses, organize tournaments, and conduct meetings—in short, they learned how to take responsibility and to be accountable without the help or hindrance of their elders. The lessons learned as youth club members would prove to be invaluable during their future years as responsible adults.

With the rapid growth of youth club teams, the former home-and-home format of competition initiated by the Mangos expanded into weekend tournaments—which now were being held almost monthly. The athletic tournaments proved to be healthy outlets for many young Filipino Americans—who, because of their relative short stature and socioeconomic circumstances, were not always able to compete on their high school teams.[10]

Tournaments were also beneficial to young Filipinas as it brought a virtual end to the strict over-protective practices of parents regarding their unmarried Bridge Generation girls. Previously, it was almost impossible for girls to venture out. Since going to tournaments was a group event with everyone piling into the few cars that were available, Filipino parents concluded there was safety in numbers and allowed girls to travel to the various athletic venues. As dramatic as this change may have been, the girls' sudden freedom represented a quantum leap from the treatment of the dalagas of the mid-1930s and early 1940s. Then, young Bridge Generation Filipinas were usually chaperoned when going out socially.

Athletic tourneys, often entailing a trip of 100 miles, were an adventure in themselves. At the time, only few youth had access to automobiles. Thus, it was not unusual for 8-10 youth to squeeze into cars. Finding a place to change into proper attire for the evening awards dances was also challenging. Those who had relatives in cities and towns sponsoring the tournaments often prevailed on them to accommodate a dozen or so young people. Consistent with Filipino tradition, out-of-town relatives were extremely hospitable, not only by providing places to change and primp for the dance but also by providing food and refreshments for the hungry youth. For those unable to have the use of a private residence, a nearby gas station had to suffice. More often than not, youth chipped in for inexpensive Chinese food eaten family-style where *bituka* (pig belly) and steamed rice could feed a carload of young people.

Teams brought their own rooting sections, primarily female fans—bringing a coed flair to the tournaments. It was inevitable that girls soon fielded their own teams. Among distaff teams were the San Francisco Mangoettes, Sacramento Static Six, Fremont Boloettes, Isleton LVM (Luzon, Visayas, and Mindinao), Livingston Dragonettes, Bay Area Bay-O-Nets, Stockton Karaans (old-timers), Stockton Filettes, Walnut Grove Bachelorettes, Concord Tomatoes, Pittsburg Islandettes, Stockton Blue Devils, Antioch Rascalettes, and the Isleton Hawkettes.

The emergence of female teams in the mid '50s came too late for some athletically inclined girls. Virginia Garcia Randall remembers practicing with brothers Jimmy and Sammy on the Salinas basketball team as they prepared for tournament play during the late '40s. What was her recollection of her abilities? She was as good as some of the players.[11]

With the rapid growth of youth clubs, came team competition in volleyball and softball. Volleyball attracted a number of Manong Generation players who were still agile enough to compete against much younger Bridge Generation players. It was a game in which manongs excelled during their years of working in the Hawaiian sugar plantations. Younger Filipinos looked in awe at the athleticism of their elders and could only wonder how good the manongs must have been in their own youth. Fittingly, a manong, Constancio "Tanciong" Lapez of Vallejo, in his late fifties, was named most valuable player at the Bethel Island (Delta) annual volleyball tournament in 1959.

Volleyball proved to be highly popular for female teams as competition could often be more intense than that involving male youth. Nina Dublin Gonzalez, of the Livingston Dragonettes, vividly recalls a grueling, hard fought tournament, "I can still remember how the whole team lay sprawled on the ground from sheer exhaustion for several minutes after winning the championship."[12]

Teams fielded by the Filipino-Mango Athletic Club of San Francisco dominated basketball competition for years. Initially led by Babe Samson, Dixon Campos, Joe San Felipe, and Felix Duag and followed in later years by high school stars Art Suguitan, Rudy Delphino, and Rudy Calica, the Mangos were in a class by themselves. Softball was the domain of the Livingston Dragons with their overpowering pitching staff of Sonny and Fred Pomicpic, and Hank Dacuyan. Led by the Galanida brothers, Jimmy and Dave, and the four Gemoya brothers, Mo, Tony, Pat, and "Big Boy", the Fremont Bolos were among the teams usually vying for volleyball championships.

The athletic tournaments were a popular venue for Filipino young people and attracted scores of non-players in addition to the athletes and their female rooters. The social highlight was the Saturday night awards dance when trophies were awarded to winning clubs. Players and non-players alike mingled freely with those from other communities. Fred Basconcillo recalls that as a teenager: "We loved the tournament dances, because it gave the chance for us younger guys to check out the girls from the other towns."[13]

The athletic tourneys and the awards dances that followed not only provided the opportunity to check out one another, it also provided Bridge Generation youth a rare opportunity to socialize with out of town counterparts. Good natured ribbing, especially among the boys, was commonplace. The big city Mangos were kidded about being dressed in the latest styles—cashmere sweaters and spit-shined shoes—while the t-shirt and Levi's clad country boys from Livingston were teased for being readily identified by the ever present dust on their scuffed-up shoes. Considering that these young people did not grow up together, lived many miles apart, and usually saw one another only at tournaments, they got along surprisingly well. Perhaps Bridge Generation youth learned the Filipino value of pakikisama (smooth personal relations) from their parents. In any event, serious disagreements on the athletic courts and fields were rare; and fights at dances were virtually nonexistent.

Tournaments were a time for Bridge Generation young people to socialize, make new friends, and for some—a time to meet their future husbands or wives. It was a time to expand their networks beyond the city enclaves and scattered rural communities of their home towns. It was a time to share common experiences of growing up in an America that was not always friendly to Filipinos. It was a time to learn that they had common beliefs. It was a time to share assimilation experiences in their struggles between the traditional values of their parents and the popular culture of American contemporary life. It was a time to continue developing their own unique identity as Filipino Americans. It was a time to come together as members of the Bridge Generation.

During the 1960s the number of Filipino youth clubs drastically declined. A major reason for the decline was the prohibitive cost of insurance that was now required by local schools and municipalities to hold tournaments in their gymnasiums. But the most significant factor was that social and recreational activities were now open to Filipino youth in what was now a more ethnically enlightened and open America—activities that formerly were closed to the Bridge Generation.[14]

The Filipino-Mango Athletic Club of San Francisco, the very first youth club, was one of the first to cease operations. Many of its original members had grown too old to compete or had moved out of the Fillmore District neighborhood. A greater reason for the decline of the Mangos was the changing character of the Filipino community as a result of the Immigration and Nationality Act of 1965 which greatly increased the number of Philippine immigrants—limited to only fifty persons per year by the Tydings-McDuffie Act of 1934.

> The Filipino American community became predominantly first generation immigrant which shifted the community focus from American based issues to Philippine issues. These new immigrants defined Filipino as someone who knew the language and culture of the Philippines. These new immigrants set up their own organizations and had little interest in the earlier established groups. Thus recruitment into the Filipino Mango Club ceased. Many of the Bridge

Generation felt alienated by the new immigrants and withdrew into their old established networks.[15]

The decline of youth clubs was met with mixed feelings by the Bridge Generation. While thankful that young Filipino Americans now had more opportunities to participate in American social and recreational life, it was difficult to accept that Filipino youth clubs—healthy outlets for the Bridge Generation for so many years—were no longer part of the Filipino youth experience.

The youth club movement was not unique to the Bridge Generation. Other ethnic groups established their own clubs through which they were able to develop their own ethnic identity and sub-culture. As previously noted, San Francisco Chinese and Japanese American youth regularly competed in an All-Oriental tournament. In California's Central Valley, most communities boasted Japanese American softball teams. The experience of second generation Mexican-Americans strikingly parallels that of the Bridge Generation. After researching George J. Sanchez' book "Becoming Mexican American: Ethnicity, Culture and Identity in Chicano Los Angeles," Annalissa Arangcon Herbert writes:

> Like the Chicano youth, the Filipino youth sought to find a balance between the American and the Filipino sides of their identities. Like the Filipino youth, Chicanos developed various youth organizations exclusively for other Chicanos. . . . Furthermore, like other Filipinos, the Chicano youths saw themselves as a part of the American system but did not feel that this necessarily conflicted with their appreciation for their Mexican heritage.[16]

As noted at the beginning of this chapter, participation in an ethnic based (youth) club can have a positive effect on the self-esteem of its participants. Herbert's study also concluded that the following benefits, while based on the Mangos' experience in San Francisco, can be generalized to apply to all Bridge Generation youth club participants.[17]

- tournaments gathered youth into a critical mass which helped develop a group identity
- social events gave Filipino youth a setting where they felt they belonged
- a support network was created of young Filipinos who shared the same concerns, had common ties to a single ethnicity, and faced the same hardships
- youth clubs contributed to developing their own specific identity by creating the rationale between traditional Filipino culture and American society
- clubs consisting of their peers were a nurturing environment and a haven from prejudice
- the self-sustaining operation of clubs was a leadership training ground for future success

There was another benefit accruing to participants. The camaraderie and lasting friendships developed with youth clubs gained in importance as they grew older. For example, it was not unusual to call on old friends at the last minute after not seeing them for decades or even if their friends lived hundreds of miles away. This was a source of bewilderment for the children of Bridge Generation Filipinos who would never think of descending on their own friends with little advance notice.

The youth clubs of the 1940s-50s appear to validate Herbert's conclusion that affiliation with youth clubs can have a positive effect on the self-esteem of its participants. Similarly supported are the postulates in Chapter One by Revilla—that ethnic identity is the product of our historical backgrounds and the process of negotiating and constructing a life in the United States—and that of Yen Le Espiritu who theorizes Bridge Generation Filipino Americans created a culture that is neither the culture of their parents or that of American society but includes elements of both at the same time.

Notes

1. Annalissa Arangcon Herbert *Growing Up in America: The Filipino-Mango Athletic Club of San Francisco 1938-1955* (unpublished thesis, UCLA, 1996), p. 69.
2. Ibid., p. 35.
3. Ibid., pp. 45-46.
4. Philippine News, January 10-16, 1974.
5. Dixon Campos *Recollections* in Souvenir Booklet, Grand Reunion: Filipino American Athletic Clubs, 1991, p. 7.
6. Herbert, p. 8.
7. Herb Jamero *History of the Livingston Fil-American Youth Club* in Luna M. Jamero ed. *Talk Story: Anthology of Stories by Filipino Americans of the Central Valley of California* Filipino American National Historical Society, Central Valley Chapter (Merced, CA: Carpenter Printing, 2008), p. 72.
8. Grand Reunion II, Souvenir Booklet, 1997, p. 2.
9. Ibid., p. 2.
10. Peter Jamero *Growing Up Brown: Memoirs of a Filipino American* (Seattle: University of Washington Press, 2006), p. 76.
11. Virginia Garcia Randall interview, June 19, 2008.
12. Nina Dublin Gonzalez interview, April 8, 2008.
13. Fred Basconcillo interview in Herbert, p. 49.
14. Jamero, p. 159.
15. Herbert, p. 63.
16. Ibid., p. 24.
17. Ibid., pp. 69-70.

4. In America's Workforce

> *By 1970, there was already a shift from working-class to professional occupations. Over one fourth (26.8%) of Filipinos in 1970 were in managerial, professional, and technical occupations. Almost one fifth (18.9%) were in sales or clerical positions. Nevertheless, the largest proportion, one third (33.5%) were service workers and farmworkers.*
>
> U.S. Department of Health, Education, and Welfare[1]

BACKGROUND

The *manong* generation was largely recruited during the 1920-30s to meet critical farm labor demands in American agriculture. American recruiters particularly targeted young Filipinos from the poor regions of the Ilocos and Visayan provinces in the Philippines, where hard work was a tradition. Most had minimal education. All had a young person's sense of adventure and a strong sense of wanting to contribute to the well-being of their families.

For most of their years in America the *manong* generation was relegated to the lowest paying jobs. They worked as farm laborers, Alaskan cannery workers, and domestics; and in jobs not requiring extensive education such as music and service jobs with unions, restaurants, and as stewards in the U.S. Navy. Most were employed in menial work. Illustrative of the *manong* generation's occupations are the following categories in Fred Cordova's landmark pictorial essay "Filipinos: Forgotten Asian Americans": Agriculture/Sakadas, Agriculture/California Migrant Stream, Alaska Canneries, U.S. Navy, Music, Professional Sports, and Unexpected Work and Businesses.[2] Despite being relegated to the lowest echelon of the American work force, however, the values of hard work and family responsibility, inspired the *manong* generation to "maintain high labor-force participation rates" throughout their history in the United States.[3]

With the favorable economy of post-war America, many members of the Bridge Generation opted to enter the labor market as high school graduates.[4] While entrenched discriminatory practices in the workplace were often formidable barriers in seeking employment, new products in industry and the beginning growth of the service sector economy provided increased opportunities for work. As noted above, the traditions of a strong work ethic and high workforce participation of their *manong* generation parents were additional incentives for seeking work. Those factors, plus the continuing American trend of marrying early, combined to find increased numbers of the Bridge Generation in the world of work.

The end of World War II also sparked an unprecedented increase in the enrollment of Bridge Generation Filipinos in colleges, universities, and technical schools—thanks to the GI Bill. The visionary federal legislation provided the necessary wherewithal that enabled thousands of veterans, including Filipino Americans, to get a college education and/or other training. At the same time, the full employment economy during the war years enabled *manong* generation parents to save for their children's education, thus opening the door for non-veteran Filipino Americans to enter college and training in greater numbers as well.

In prior years, Filipino families were content to have their Bridge Generation children finish high school, seldom having the resources for additional training. Seeing them enrolled in institutions of higher learning and in technical schools was like having a dream come true. *Manong* generation parents immigrated to the United States to chase the American Dream. Education and training were seen as ways that would lead to a better life. Because of the debilitating effects of the Great Depression and discrimination, however, that dream was often elusive and unattainable. Now, the GI Bill and a strong post-war economy gave them hope. Their children had a greater chance of going to college and/or getting specialized training. Perhaps their American dream would become a reality after all—if not for them—for their Bridge Generation children. They looked to the day when their children would have an easier life than they experienced.

At the end of World War II, the Bridge Generation had either reached or was approaching adulthood. Like all young people, they began the uncertain process of navigating their way through the maze of America's workforce. Would they, by 1970, be represented among the one-fourth (26.8%) of Filipinos in managerial, professional, and technical occupations, or one-fifth (18.9%) in sales or clerical positions, or one-third (33.5%) service workers or farmworkers reported by Lott above? This chapter will examine the Bridge Generation in the world of work.

"WHO'S WHO AMONG BRIDGE GENERATION FILIPINO AMERICANS" PROJECT

It is difficult, at best, to assess the degree of participation and impact of an ethnic group in American society. When a group has not had the benefit of empirical data, however, the difficulty is compounded. As noted earlier, a comprehensive study on the Bridge Generation has never been conducted. To date Filipino American researchers have turned their backs on the Bridge Generation, choosing instead to focus its attention on the generation preceding it—the *manong* generation—and the one generation that followed—those Filipinos who flocked to America in the wake of the liberalized Immigration and Nationality Act of 1965.

Two Filipino American National Historical Society (FANHS) initiatives are believed to be the only existing documents providing pertinent labor force information dealing exclusively with the Bridge Generation. While the efforts did not undergo the scholarly rigor of a research study, the documents do offer glimpses into the Bridge Generation's workforce participation. The first—the uncompleted 1998 Central Valley Chapter's "Who's Who Among Bridge Generation Filipino Americans" project—attracted 105 respondents who provided demographic data on a variety of subjects. The following findings in the *Career/Employment* category are of particular significance in our examination of workforce participation:

- 73 (72%) of the respondents worked in white collar jobs
- 23 (21%) were in blue collar positions
- 6 (4%) were homemakers
- 3 (2%) were in music

Among other data reported in the Who's Who initiative:

- Average number of children in their parent's families—6
- Average number of children in their own families—3
- 79% reported obtaining some college education or training beyond high school
- 20% reported obtaining some high school education
- 1 respondent reported having a grade school education
- 100 respondents declared "Catholic" as religious preference
- 95% declared themselves as "Democratic" in their political affiliation

VIP AWARDS

The second FANHS initiative providing a glimpse into the workforce participation of the Bridge Generation was the 1994 VIP (Very Important *Pinoy/Pinay*) Awards for lifetime achievement. The awards were a highlight of the FANHS Fifth National Conference held in San Francisco which had as its theme, "Honoring the Bridge Generation: Sons and Daughters of Filipino Pioneers." In preparation for the awards, nominations were first solicited from FANHS chapters. Fifty-four (54) nominations were submitted from across the country. Nominations were then judged by a panel of non-Filipino American academicians based on two criteria relating to the nominees' contributions to: (1) their field or profession and (2) their Filipino American experience. Finally, FANHS' board president and executive director screened the panel's selections to assure adherence to criteria (2).

Considering that the awards were for lifetime achievement, it is recognized that nominations may be biased to favor achievements in professions and pop-culture fields. Nevertheless, the findings provide a rare glimpse into the Bridge Generation's participation in America's workforce. Below is a compilation of the nominees' professions/fields in descending order followed by pertinent observations:

Category	Number	Percentage (rounded)
Arts	9	18
Education	9	18
Public Service	6	12
Community Service	6	12
Executive	5	9
Health/Human Services	5	9
Military	4	7
Athletics	4	7
Elected Official	2	4
Science	2	4
Legal	1	2
Communications	1	2

- At first glance the high percentage of respondents under the Arts category in the VIP Awards may be surprising. Upon closer observation, however, all but two respondents are in the field of Music—a field that requires natural talent but not necessarily advanced education or training. Perhaps as important, it is a field that has strong appeal to the cultural traditions of rhythm-loving Filipinos. The fact that they are all jazz musicians is also significant as their music continues to reflect the bop musical style in vogue during their growing up years pioneered by such artists as Charlie Parker, Dizzy Gillespie, Miles Davis, and Dave Brubeck.
- The 9% for the two Executive categories also may be surprising. While future follow-ups of the category should be more definitive, the speculation here is that the modest percentage is a positive reflection on slowly but steadily increasing opportunities in Bridge Generation participation in American life.
- On the other hand, the prominence of Education in the Who's Who study is not surprising for Bridge Generation Filipino Americans. A

strong cultural belief in the value of education plus the motivation to come to America of many of their immigrant parents to obtain further education are both seen as providing the impetus to pursue education as a career.
- The percentages in the categories of Public Service, Health/Human Services, and Military are assumed to reflect the relative openness of these fields to ethnic minorities. While most of the respondents were already too entrenched in their chosen fields to personally benefit by the time that affirmative action legislation was enacted in the 1970s, the availability of civil service protections appears to have been a significant factor in the Bridge Generation's initial choices for employment.
- Much like Music, Athletics represents a category requiring natural talent. But unlike music, excelling in the category also requires competing with taller and larger individuals of other ethnic groups, which is surmised as the reason for its lower participation rate.
- The scarcity of Bridge Generation participation in the workforce categories of Science and Legal, in all likelihood, represents the relative difficulty of Bridge Generation Filipino Americans to obtain the advanced education necessary to enter those fields. The total absence of physicians in the VIP Awards data suggests the same difficulty.
- The high participation rate in the Community Service category is considered as efforts to deal more effectively with the needs of the Filipino community—needs which often inspired Bridge Generation individuals to work towards providing critical services for their communities.

SELECTED BIOGRAPHICAL SKETCHES

At this point, it may be of interest to readers to put some faces behind the categories and numbers. Below are brief sample descriptions of Bridge Generation individuals falling within the aforementioned workforce categories. The sample descriptions roughly parallel the workforce categories with the highest Bridge Generation participation as reflected in the FANHS VIP initiative.

Arts—Music:

- A native of Hilo HI, Filipino-Japanese American *Gabe Baltazar* first received national attention as lead alto saxophonist for the Stan Kenton orchestra in 1960, a position he held for three years. During the late '60s he played in Los Angeles area studio bands with the ABC, CBS, and NBC networks backing the Tonight Show, Laugh-In, Pat Boone Show, Jerry Lewis Show, among others.
- Born in 1932 in San Pedro, California and raised in Oakland, *Evangeline Canonizado Buell* is an accomplished folk guitarist and singer having performed with Harry Belafonte, The Kingston Trio, and The Limelighters. A longtime board member of FANHS, her autobiography *Twenty-five Chickens and a Pig for a Bride* was published in 2006.

- *Primo Kim* (nee Villarruz) grew up in San Jose, California before launching his musical career as a vocalist-pianist in the early '60s. A Seattle resident since 1971, he has enjoyed extended popularity at regular gigs in such venues as the Edgewater Hotel, Olympic Hotel, and Daniel's Lake Washington Restaurant. Kim has also extensively performed in New York City, Las Vegas, and the Bay Area.
- During the 1960s pianist *Mike Montano* toured America, Europe, and Asia as accompanist and main foil for comedian Jack E. Leonard. He subsequently settled in Las Vegas where he served as music director at the Flamingo Hotel and Casino. As a teenager in his native Stockton, California, Montano was the leader and arranger for an all-Filipino American vocal and instrumental group.
- *Joseph "Flip" Nunez*, perhaps the foremost jazz pianist, singer, and composer of Filipino ancestry, got his musical start in Los Angeles' Central Avenue during the late '40s, sitting in with such bop stars as Dexter Gordon. It was in the Bay Area, however, where he became best known, performing in such jazz clubs as the Rickshaw in the '50s, Bop City in the '60s, and Pearl's in the '70s to mid '90s.
- The musical *Tenio family* grew up in Stockton where they honed their jazz and pop music talents before going on to perform throughout California. Jimmy, the eldest and a World War II veteran with the Army's First Filipino Regiment, played tenor and alto saxophone. Joe played the drums when he was not playing basketball for the local youth club, while the two youngest—Josie and Rudy, vocalists and pianists—also performed as a duo and as soloists.

Performing Arts:

- Raised in Oakdale and San Jose California, *Pacita Todtod Bobadilla* is best known for her singing role in the World War II movie They Were Expendable, starring John Wayne—the first Filipina American to be featured in a major Hollywood film. Perhaps her most important role, however, was in helping to initiate a successful petition to the U.S. Secretary of Army in 1942 to establish an all-Filipino regiment during World War II.
- *Jose De Vega* was born in 1934 in San Diego, the son of a Filipino father and a Colombian mother. He was the first Filipino American to gain prominence in Broadway theater and in motion pictures for his portrayal of Chino in the hit musical West Side Story. Following his breakthrough performances on the stage and in movies, Joe made numerous appearances as a television actor, director, dancer, and choreographer.

Education:

- *Myron Mays Apilado* was born and raised in Chicago, the son of a Filipino immigrant and an African American mother. He has had a distinguished educational career including serving twelve years as the Vice President of Minority Affairs at the University of Washington. He was the keynote speaker at the FANHS National Conference in Chicago in 1992.
- An original member of the Livingston Filipino American Youth Association "Dragons", *Henry Dacuyan* rose to the position of assistant principal for the Campbell School District in suburban San Jose, California. In the mid '80s he returned to his hometown of Winton to teach. After retiring, he served several terms on the local school board.
- Born in the small Central Valley community of Selma, California, *Ronald Dangaran* rose through the education ranks to become Superintendent of the Merced City School District from 1985-90. In 1993 he was elected to the Board of Education for the Fresno Unified School District—a district with an enrollment of 78,000 students.
- A member of the first Filipino youth club—the Filipino-Mango Athletic Club of San Francisco—*Felix Duag* spent his entire educational career with the San Francisco School District where he was a teacher, principal, area manager and superintendent, and coordinator of public information and public affairs.
- Upon seeing action in the Philippines during WWII, Hawaii native *Domingo Los Banos* promised God that if he survived he would become a teacher. He kept his promise as he went to Columbia University, taught, and eventually became a superintendent of schools on Oahu. He was the moving force behind the 2005 PBS documentary An Untold Triumph, the story of the First and Second Filipino Regiments.
- An award winning and internationally recognized scholar, *Barbara Mercedes Posadas* has been a professor of history at Northern Illinois University since 1974. A prolific researcher, most notable have been her publications on the history of Filipinos in the Midwest. She has lectured extensively in the United States as well as France and the Philippines.
- *Andres "Sonny" Tangalin* rose from a grade school teacher in the Seattle School District to become supervisor for compensatory programs, a high school vice principal, and principal at the elementary, alternative, and high school levels. He also served as department head of instructional services for the local educational service district that provided support to more than thirty school districts.

Athletics:

- After a long minor league baseball career with the Seattle Rainiers where he was named Most Popular Player in 1955, speedy centerfielder

- *Bobby Balcena*, a native of Long Beach, California, became the first Filipino to play major league baseball when he was called up by the Cincinnati Reds in 1956.
- As a teenager *Dick Dagampat* played for a Los Angeles area Filipino youth club team that went undefeated in winning the youth club tournament championship in Stockton in the early '50s. As a young man, he was the starting fullback for the U.S. Naval Academy football team from 1956-58, which culminated in being named team captain in his senior year.
- Often called an uncrowned champion, *Bernard Docusen* challenged Sugar Ray Robinson for the world welterweight title in 1948 but lost in 15 rounds in a hotly contested bout. Born in New Orleans in 1927 of a Filipino father and Creole mother, he won the AAU bantamweight title when he was 14 years of age and turned pro at 15. He was inducted into the California Hall of Fame in 2008.
- At the 1948 Olympics in London, *Vicki Manalo Draves* became the first person of Filipino ancestry to win gold—winning two gold medals for platform and springboard diving. Her path to victory was not without problems, however, as she encountered racial discrimination when she was barred from using a hotel pool in her native San Francisco.
- The son of an immigrant Filipino railroad worker and a Caucasian mother, Wilmington, North Carolina native *Roman Gabriel* was a two-time All-American quarterback at North Carolina State, breaking 22 school records in the process. He played sixteen seasons from 1962-73 as an NFL quarterback for the Los Angeles Rams and Philadelphia Eagles and was selected four times as All-Pro.

Health/Human Services:

- A registered nurse, *Deanna Daclan Balantac* was the first Filipina American to be tenured as full professor at California State University Sacramento—achieving that distinction in 1974. A member of the United Filipino Youth Club of Stockton, California, she later became co-founder and long time board member of the Associated Filipino Organizations of San Joaquin County.
- In 1961 Stockton born *Jose Fidel* was the first person of Filipino ancestry to practice dentistry in his hometown. A graduate of the University of California at Berkeley, Dr. Fidel received his DDS degree in 1959 from Creighton University in Nebraska. He is past president of the San Joaquin Dental Society. He was selected to the Edison High School Hall of Fame in 1990.
- *Royal Morales* was born in America but became stranded in the Philippines as a youth at the onset of World War II. The co-founder of the respected youth-serving agency SIPA (Search to Involve Pilipino Americans) in 1972, Royal went on to serve as executive director of a Los

Angeles based substance abuse agency from 1982 to 1994 and to teach Filipino/Asian American History at UCLA.
- The highest ranking Bridge Generation Filipino American in President Clinton's administration, *Bob Santos* served as Northwest Representative for the U.S. Department of Housing and Urban Development. The long time executive director of Inter*Im—the leading community development agency in Seattle's International/Chinatown District—he continues to work in that capacity on a part-time basis.

Military:

- A highly respected member of the Filipino-Mango Athletic Club of San Francisco, *Antonio "Dixon" Campos* later served with the U.S. Army's First Filipino Regiment during World War II, receiving a bronze medal for valor. He became a full colonel in the Army Reserves in 1979.
- *Vince Cobalis*, an early member of the Mangos, became a career army man after initially seeing action in the Philippines with the First Filipino Regiment during World War II and later in the Korean War, when he was a prisoner of war. He retired as a Chief Warrant Officer and currently resides in El Paso, Texas.
- After attending Brown Military Academy of San Diego in the early 1940s, Bay Area native *William Diangson* saw active duty with the U.S. Army. He went on to serve with the California National Guard, attaining the rank of Brigadier General.

Elected Official:

- The first U.S. state governor of Filipino ancestry, *Ben Cayetano* was the fifth governor of the State of Hawaii, serving two terms from 1994-2002 before he was termed out. He also has the distinction of being the first Filipino American Lieutenant Governor. Raised by his father, Cayetano was a latchkey child growing up in the tough Honolulu neighborhood of Kalihi.
- *Edwardo Malapit* was elected for four consecutive two-year terms as Mayor of Kauai, Hawaii, beginning in 1974. He holds the distinction of being the first Filipino American mayor of any United States municipality. As mayor, he is credited with improving and updating Kauai's infrastructure. Prior to becoming mayor, he served on the Kauai County Council for eight years.
- Attorney *Dolores Estigoy Sibonga* became the first Filipina to serve on a major metropolitan city council when she was appointed to the Seattle City Council in 1979. Subsequently, she was elected to two additional terms to serve a total of twelve years on the Council. This was not her first "Filipino First." In 1973 she was the first person of Filipino ancestry to pass the Washington State Bar.

Science:

- A nuclear chemist, *James Fontanilla* spent most of his career with the Department of Energy where he was involved in the testing of radioactive gases following underground nuclear detonations. He served in the U.S. Army during the Korean War as a Second Lieutenant and remained in the reserves, attaining the rank of full colonel.
- Architect *Benjamin Santos*, born in 1938 in Los Angeles to a Filipino father and Caucasian mother, has made remarkable contributions in automobile and architectural design. Among his designs: the body of the 1961 Buick Riviera, the vehicle for the Bay Area Rapid Transit, and shopping centers in Paris, France; Vancouver, British Columbia; Anchorage, Alaska; and Palos Verde and El Cerrito, Califonia.

Public Service:

- Born in Chicago in 1941 of a Filipino father and Polish mother, *Ticiang Diangson* continues to work as Manager of the City of Seattle's Solid Waste Recycling Program, the first of its kind in the nation. She is also an active Asian American feminist and was a founding member of the Asian Pacific Women's Caucus.
- *Florence Price Duldulao* was born in Arizona but moved to San Francisco when she was two. She held executive positions at San Francisco's Mount Zion Hospital and Medical Center as Human Resource Development Director and Personnel Director.

Executive—Labor:

- When *Fred Basconcillo* was elected President of the Iron Workers Union, Local 790 in San Francisco in 1979, he became the first Filipino American to be elected president of a building and construction trades union. As president he was instrumental in changing eligibility requirements for apprenticeship programs making it possible for Filipinos and other minorities to participate.

Executive—Business:

- *Arthur Suguitan* served as Administrative Officer and Special Assistant to the Chancellor of the California State University—the largest system of higher education in the nation. He also held positions of Senior Vice President for Finance of United Way of Los Angeles and Administrative Officer of the San Francisco Cow Palace.

Communications:

- *Sumi Hara* (nee Mildred Sevilla), born in New Jersey and raised in Colorado, is a writer, journalist, poet, actress, and producer. She has been performing arts coordinator for the City of Los Angeles and an officer and member of the national board of the Screen Actors Guild since 1974.

Community Service:

- While the category is now well represented by many other Bridge Generation Filipino Americans, *Fred and Dorothy Laigo Cordova* remain in a class by themselves. They co-founded the Filipino American National Historical Society which continues to be the only historical organization focusing solely on the Filipino experience in America. Stockton-born Fred was FANHS' first board president while Dorothy, a native of Seattle, has served as executive director since its inception in 1984. In its 25 years of existence the organization has now grown to 25 chapters nationwide. FANHS was not their only joint venture. In 1957 they co-founded the Filipino Youth Activities of Seattle providing comprehensive services for Filipino American youth. And in 1974 they simultaneously received appointments as affiliate assistant professors of history at the University of Washington.

FINDINGS AND IMPLICATIONS

As reflected by the 79% reporting at least some college and the 72% working in white collar jobs in the two FANHS initiatives, the level of educational achievement and workforce participation of the Bridge Generation greatly exceeded that of their parents' *Manong* Generation—a generation with only minimal education and largely relegated to the lowest paying jobs. What was not reported is also significant—no one declared their employment to be that of farm worker or domestic.

At the same time, it must be remembered that the workforce findings of the initiatives, while interesting, only provided relatively small samples. Thus, the findings are only glimpses and are far from definitive. Secondly, the workforce categories or the time frames of the initiatives do not match that of U.S. Department of Health, Education, and Welfare's information reported by Lott above to provide clear comparisons. Moreover, as previously noted the initiatives are not studies and have not been subjected to the rigors of scholarly research. Finally, the narrow focus on workforce participation does not even begin to address the larger question of the scope and impact of the Bridge Generation's participation in the broader American mainstream. Regardless of these limitations, the overall implication of the findings is that Bridge Generation Filipino Americans, despite improved access to educational opportunities, have been and continue to be underrepresented in the nation's professions and occupations.

As for the Bridge Generation's achievements described under the Biographical Sketches section—these are modest accomplishments at best. Among the "Filipino Firsts" achieved during the 1970s, for example, were a tenured university professor, an airlines pilot, the president of a local union, a colonel in the Army Reserves, and a department director.[5] While laudable, all of the identified professional or occupational achievements were at modest levels—by any measure. Moreover, most of the recognitions were for accomplishments by the "Filipino First" achievers when they were already in their fifties or sixties. To this day the ranks of the Bridge Generation, with only rare exceptions, do not include a CEO of a major corporation, a member of Congress, or artists, engineers, scientists, or attorneys well-known to the broader American mainstream. Even heavily Filipino-populated California has never been represented in the state assembly or the senate. In comparison, second generation members of other Asian groups—the Japanese Nisei, and Chinese, Korean, Vietnamese, and Indian counterparts—have made a greater impact in American society and at a far faster pace.

Again, the clear challenge is for academia to conduct a comprehensive review of the Bridge Generation while there are still a significant number of surviving members to study.

Notes

1. U.S. Department of Health, Education, and Welfare in Juanita Tamayo Lott "Demographic Changes Transforming the Filipino American Community" in Maria P.P. Root ed. *Filipino Americans: Transformation and Identity* (Thousand Oaks, CA: Sage Publications, 1997), p.17. By 1970 the Bridge Generation was in their 40s, 50s, and 60s—prime years of employment.

2. Fred Cordova *Filipinos, Forgotten Asian Americans: A Pictorial Essay, 1763-circa 1963* (Dubuque, IA: Kendall/Hunt Publishers, 1983), p. vi.

3. Juanita Tamayo Lott *Common Destiny: Filipino American Generations* (Lanham, MD: Bowman and Littlefield Publishers Inc., 2006, p. 35.

4. Lott, p. 50.

5. Peter Jamero *Growing Up Brown: Memoirs of a Filipino American* (Seattle: University of Washington Press, 2006), 1998, pp. 306-7.

5. Civic Participation

The best way to find yourself is to lose yourself in the service of others.

Mohandes Gandhi[1]

As noted earlier, Juanita Tamayo Lott paid tribute to what she calls the "silent generation" (i.e., Bridge Generation) for its involvement in various aspects of American society.[2] Lott also observes:

> For Filipino American generations, what they continue to contribute toward the common destiny of multi-generational Americans are their renowned skills of caring and hospitality, and the interpersonal skills rooted in their Filipino heritage and nurtured in full civic participation in the United States of America.[3]

This chapter will concern itself with Bridge Generation civic participation. For purposes of this discussion, civic participation is defined as the Bridge Generation's access to education, serving in the military, voting, and engaging in social/labor activism.[4] Its record in the various aspects of civic participation is mixed. Education, military service, and voting have had a strong response from the Bridge Generation while the response to social/labor activism has been lukewarm.

EDUCATION

From the Filipino parents of the Bridge Generation came a strong belief in the value of education, reinforced by Thomasite[5] teachers who helped spread an American-style public school system throughout the Philippines at the turn of the 20th century. Some immigrated to America to further their education. Many others came for the economic benefits they understood would be available for them. And when their objectives were thwarted in America, they looked to their children to fulfill their dreams through education and a better life. As reported in the FANHS initiative in the last chapter, seventy-nine percent (79%) of Bridge Generation respondents achieved at least some education beyond high school—thanks to a strong economy and the enactment of the GI Bill. Their ensuing high participation level in education appears to be a clear indication that the Bridge Generation met the dreams of their immigrant parents.

MILITARY SERVICE

As has been seen in the findings of the FANHS initiatives, the military also had a high Bridge Generation participation rate. Nowhere was this more dramatically demonstrated than in the immediate hours after the Japanese bombed Pearl Harbor on December 7, 1941. Virtually overnight, Filipino Americans throughout the West Coast and Hawaii enlisted in the various armed services and in the merchant marine. The onset of the Korean War in 1950 brought a similar response from the Bridge Generation.

The young men were not solely motivated by wartime patriotism. For them as well as for their parents, joining the military was also a public validation that they were Americans. No longer should they be considered as unwelcome foreigners as many of them had previously experienced. On a more practical level, they also were motivated to enlist by their realization that military service was one of the relatively few occupations open to Filipino Americans.

Military involvement was not limited to active duty. At the end of World War II many soldiers, sailors, and airmen opted to join home town reserve units. In post-war San Francisco the local army reserve unit consisted of many Bridge Generation Filipino Americans—most of them former members of the Filipino-Mango youth club.

VOTING

Filipino parents of the Bridge Generation arrived in the United States as "nationals." While they were not aliens nor required to hold passports, neither were they given the right to vote. Voting rights were not to come until 1952 but only after enduring years of discrimination, racism, and second class citizenship in America. As a consequence, citizenship and the right to vote were very dear to these Filipino immigrants. The conferring of citizenship would confirm that Filipino immigrants would now be "real Americans". In the immediate aftermath of the implementing legislation, they flocked to U.S. Immigration Offices to apply for citizenship. Many studied for citizenship tests with the help of their children who, in turn, personally experienced the passion and importance that citizenship and voting held for their parents. After taking the oath of allegiance, the Manong Generation, like immigrants from other countries, was among the most reliable and faithful of American voters. Inspired by the example of their parents, voting age members of the Bridge Generation too could be counted upon to vote at every ensuing local, state, and federal election.

Running for elected office would appear to be a logical next step for such a high participant voting group. However, the Bridge Generation has not been heavily involved as candidates. Outside of Hawaii with its large Filipino population, it is rare to find an elected official from this generation. A few have run but only one has ever been elected to an office in a major metropolitan community—Dolores Sibonga who served several terms on the Seattle City Council. And to date, no one from the generation has been elected to a state or national office.

SOCIAL ACTIVISM

Beginning in the mid 1950s and into the 1960s, America experienced an unprecedented series of social activism and protest focusing largely on civil rights and the war in Vietnam. There were scattered instances of Bridge Generation activism such as Roy Morales and Al Mendoza in Los Angeles and Bob Santos and Andres "Sonny" Tangalin in Seattle. However, most Bridge Generation Filipino Americans were not visible in the social activism of the times. Why the small number of activists? After all, their parent's generation had a long history of engaging in labor strikes against poor working conditions and low pay in Hawaii and the West Coast. They were taught to be proud to be Filipino and to stand up for their rights. Several interrelated reasons are submitted for the low level of Bridge Generation participation. First, the years of social activism were during the benevolent Eisenhower era when the country's war veterans and their contemporaries were more interested in getting on with their education and employment than with social issues. Secondly, like most Americans of this same age group, the Bridge Generation was in their early years of marriage and raising children. Understandably, they placed a higher priority on their responsibilities as husbands and fathers. Third, they were now so dispersed they could not easily mobilize the requisite critical mass to make a significant difference. Unlike their youth club days when they were in relatively close proximity to one another, the post-war years found members of the Bridge Generation scattered across many more communities and states.

An exception to the relative lack of Bridge Generation activism was the Filipino Young Turks[6] of Seattle—a close-knit, politically savvy group who serendipitously came together in 1970. Bridge Generation core members were Mike Castilliano, Fred and Dorothy Cordova, Bob Flor, Roy Flores, Pete and Terri Jamero, Bob Santos, Dolores Sibonga, and Sonny Tangalin. Non-Bridge Generation Young Turks were Tony Ogilvie and Larry Flores, then in their early twenties. The only non-Filipino Young Turks were Dale Tiffany, a soft-spoken Flathead Indian married to Dorothy Cordova's sister Jeannette and Roman Catholic priest Harvey McIntyre.

The Young Turks' collective and individual strengths, particularly its ability to relate to the diverse Seattle community, were key factors to its success. Fred Cordova's various articles in Seattle's two daily newspapers through the years began the process of bringing the Filipino community's issues to the conscious attention of the city's mainstream. Bob Santos' well-publicized arrests in protest marches against discrimination in the construction industry and in the Native American take over of Fort Lawton established his credibility with all minority groups. As board president of the Filipino Youth Activities of Seattle, Inc., Terri Jamero could mobilize the collective strength of the respected organization. Sonny Tangalin built a strong track record in his work with various minority coalitions, particularly in civil rights and affirmative action issues. Central Area native Larry Flores gave the group entrée into the African American community while Dorothy Cordova, the eldest daughter of a pioneer Filipino family provided important access to the establishment Filipino community. Dolores Sibonga's election to the Seattle City Council provided the Young Turks with a spokesperson and channel in local government. In addition to serving as parish priest for most members of the Young Turks, Father McIntyre sat on the City of Seattle's Human Rights Commission. Mike Castilliano, Assistant to the Vice President for Minority Affairs, and Roy Flores, Director of the Ethnic Cultural Center, opened doors to resources at the University of Washington. Energetic Tony Ogilivie, assistant director of minority affairs at Seattle University, served as the group's idea man. Dale Tiffany brought organizational and business skills to the Young Turks while his wife Jeannette took the lead in multimedia communications. Bob Flor provided a valuable linkage to the Democratic Party and the author's long experience in federal government was critical in obtaining funding support for the group's initiatives.

From 1970 through the mid 1980s, the Young Turks would play a major role in Seattle's social and political mainstream. After early victories in bringing needed funding for programs benefiting Filipino elderly, the Young Turks turned its attention to issues of the broader Seattle community. They successfully fought for federal funding for the Demonstration Project for Asian Americans—the project that gave birth to Fred Cordova's epic pictorial essay *Filipinos: Forgotten Asian Americans* and gave Dorothy Cordova her first job outside the home as DPPA's executive director. The group's efforts brought greater access, recognition, and participation to the Filipino community as a significant force in Seattle. Subsequently, the Young Turks became heavily involved in mainstream Seattle community affairs and in politics. They were asked to serve on numerous community boards and committees; their support was sought by political candidates of both parties; and they were highly visible in local, state, and national campaigns.

The Young Turks' success went beyond Seattle. After a pan-Asian demonstration protesting the absence of culturally specific health and human service programs at the 1971 national conference of the Council of Social Work Education, they coalesced with other west coast Asian Americans to establish Mental Health Training Centers in Los Angeles and San Diego. Among their collaborators were Los Angeles Bridge Generation activists Royal Morales and Al Mendoza. Morales and Mendoza would go on to play important roles in establishing needed programs for the Filipino and Asian American communities in Los Angeles, most notably the SIPA (Search to Involve Pilipino Americans) non-profit agency and a Filipino curriculum in Asian American studies.[7]

The ease with which the Young Turks were able to effectively relate with a variety of publics is a reminder of the effective role that the Filipino value of *pakikisama* (smooth personal relationships) can play.[8] In traditional Filipino culture this value can help ensure harmony among groups and individuals. While most of the American-born Bridge Generation may not have been consciously aware of *pakikisama's* genesis or purpose, it must be assumed that the cultural value was learned from their Filipino parents. Otherwise, why is it that Filipino Americans historically have been instrumental in bringing various factions together and avoiding inter-group conflicts in minority coalitions and in the youth club athletic tournaments in California?

However, it was the next generation of Filipino Americans rather than the Bridge Generation that would take up the banner of social activism. In the late 1960s, students protested against San Francisco State and the University of Washington in Seattle for their failure to be more responsive to minority concerns. At San Francisco State, the Philippine American Collegiate Endeavor (PACE), an on-campus Filipino American organization, joined the Black Student Union in a prolonged protest in 1968 that eventually resulted in the establishment of ethnic study programs and in the aggressive recruitment of minority students. PACE was led by Filipino Americans Patrick Salaver, Ron Quidichay, Robert and Ed Ilumin, and Alex Soria—none of whom were of the Bridge Generation but of the following Baby Boomer Generation.[9] The student protest at the University of Washington took a similar form except that the Filipino American student leaders, Tony Ogilvie and the Flores brothers—Roy and Larry, represented an Asian American student coalition. Of the three Filipino Americans, Roy Flores was the only member of the Bridge Generation.

The Baby Boomer Generation did not hesitate to step up to the plate for other issues of great concern to the Filipino community. They fought for fairness in employment and access to education; they protested the tearing down of the International Hotel in San Francisco and the erection of the Kingdome in Seattle;[10] they led the anti-Marcos effort in America—all efforts in which the Bridge Generation was largely absent. Lott credited the Bridge Generation for its involvement in American society as the "bridge" between the *Manong* generation and those which followed. In much the same way, the social activism demonstrated by the Baby Boomer Generation deserves to be applauded by all Filipino Americans, regardless of their own involvement or personal views on the issues.

At the same time, it must be recognized that the activism of the Baby Boomer Generation occurred at a different time and place compared to the predecessor Bridge Generation. As previously noted in Mannheim's theory of generations, "one must consider the historical and social context in which the generations exist."[11]

LABOR ACTIVISM

Throughout their presence in America, Manong Generation Filipinos have turned to activism in labor to right the wrongs they experienced—in Hawaii's sugarcane plantations, in California's agricultural fields, and in the Alaskan salmon canneries. During the early 1920s, Filipinos led by Pablo Manlapit struck against the Hawaiian Sugar Plantation Association to protest poor living conditions and low wages.[12] Later in the decade Chris Mensalvas and Ernie Mangaoang—concerned over the disparate treatment of Filipinos in Alaska canneries—organized Filipinos into what would become Local 37 of the International Longshoremen and Warehousemen Union.[13] Rufo Canete led the Filipino Labor Union (FLU) walkout of lettuce farm workers in the Salinas Valley in 1933.[14] The grape strike of 1965 in Delano led by Larry Itliong, Philip Vera Cruz, and Pete Velasco culminated years of protest against low wages and poor living conditions by the Agricultural Workers Organizing Committee (AWOC). The AWOC would soon merge with the Cesar Chavez-led National Farm Workers Association to form the United Farm Workers.[15]

The Bridge Generation, most of whom entered the world of work after World War II, found itself in a far different workforce situation. While the great proportion of their *Manong* Generation parents worked in farm labor and domestic jobs, Bridge Generation Filipino Americans, with more employment options, were dispersed across many more occupations—continuing the full employment phenomenon during World War II when jobs formerly the domain of white men were opened to ethnic minorities and women. As a result, their participation in labor activism was neither as visible nor significant as that of the *Manong* Generation.

Regardless of greater work opportunities, the Bridge Generation encountered similar barriers in seeking and maintaining employment—ethnic discrimination, an "old boy's" employer network, and requirements unrelated to job performance. Public service, with its civil service protections, was an attractive employment choice for the Bridge Generation. At the same time, however, public service often had restrictions unrelated to the job, such as unrealistic height standards, that effectively ruled out ethnic groups, including Filipino Americans. The City of Seattle, for example, required candidates for firemen to be five-foot six inches in height—a requirement not supportable as a criterion for job performance. Asian American activists, with the strong support of Bridge Generation Bob Santos—then a member of the Seattle Human Rights Commission—were ultimately successful in overturning the requirement during the early 1970s.[16]

Unions had their own brand of unfair restrictions. Not only did they also use restrictions unrelated to job performance, but unions often kept ethnic minorities from participating in apprenticeship programs by requiring applicants to be recommended by journeymen when there were no minority journeymen to make such recommendations. In view of being widely dispersed in the workforce, Bridge Generation labor activists chose to achieve change from the inside through individual efforts, rather than through group pressure—the preferred approach used by the *Manong* Generation. They fought to eliminate requirements unrelated to job performance; circumvented barriers to apprenticeship participation by obtaining the requisite training through certified programs in technical schools and community colleges; coalesced with other minorities and women in advocating for common objectives; and formed informal communication networks with one another.

The experience of Fred Basconcillo in San Francisco is a typical example. Unable to enter an iron worker apprenticeship program because of the lack of a journeyman to recommend him, he qualified to participate as an apprentice by enrolling in a local trade school. Basconcillo's activism did not stop there. After becoming a journeyman, he threw himself into union politics and with the support of ethnic minorities and women was elected President of the San Francisco Local of the Iron Worker's Union. Subsequently, as president he was instrumental for the national union changing its eligibility requirements that enabled more minorities and women to participate in apprenticeship programs.[17]

The strategy of achieving change from within was also successfully used by other Bay Area Bridge Generation labor leaders—Francisco "Babe" Samson, President, Marine Cooks and Stewards Union; William "Bill" Daly, President, Painters Union; and Ron Anolin, West Coast Representative, Service Employees International Union. In Hawaii, where Filipinos were more concentrated, Abba Ramos rose from president of his local of the International Longshoremen and Warehousemen Union to become General Organizer in charge of the entire west coast, including Alaska and Hawaii with headquarters in San Francisco.

Notes

1. *Writings* in Elaine Bernstein Partnow *Great Quotes for all Occasions* (New York: Alpha Books, 2008).

2. Juanita Tamayo Lott *Common Destiny: Filipino American Generations* (Lanham, MD: Bowman and Littlefield Publishers Inc., 2006, p. 45.

3. Ibid., p. xi.

4. Ibid, p. 107, Lott includes education, military service, and voting in her definition of civic participation. To that list, the author adds engaging in social and labor activism.

5. Teodoro A. Agoncillo *A Short History of the Philippines* (New York and Toronto: The New American Library, 1969. Thomasites were approximately 600 American teachers, named after the ship that brought to the Philippines—the U.S.S. Thomas—who established a U.S. style public school system consisting of primary, elementary, high school, normal, trade and arts, and university levels at the turn of the 20th century.

6. Peter M. Jamero *The Filipino American Young Turks of Seattle: A Unique Experience in the American Sociopolitical Mainstream* in Maria P.P. Root ed. *Filipino Americans: Transformation and Identity* (Thousand Oaks, CA: Sage Publications, 1997), pp 299-315. The name "Young Turks" was coined by Sylvestre Tangalan, president of the Filipino Community of Seattle, who likened group's success in bringing funding to the community to that of the insurgent Turkish group of the early 1900s.

7. Royal F. Morales *Makibaka, the Pilipino American Struggle* (Los Angeles: Mountainview Publishers, 1974), pp. 100-103, 111.

8. Lott, p. 106.

9. The student leaders, all born after WW-II, are categorized as "baby boomers", as defined by Lott, p. 45.

10. Tearing down the International Hotel and erecting the Kingdome would have resulted in the displacement of elderly Filipino *manongs*.

11. Karl Mannheim "Sociology of Generations" *Essays on the Sociology of Culture* (Routledge & Paul Press, 1956).

12. Melinda Tria Kerkvliet *Pablo Manlapit's Fight For Justice* in Jonathan Y. Okamura, Amefil R. Agbayani, and Melinda Tria Kerkvliet guest eds. *Social Process in Hawaii* (University of Hawaii at Manoa, 1991), pp. 153-168.

13. Linda Espana-Maram *Creating Masculinity in Los Angeles's Little Manila* (New York: Columbia University Press, 2006), p. 47.

14. Espana-Maram, p.45.

15. Craig Scharlin and Lilia V. Villanueva *Philip Vera Cruz: A Personal History of Filipino Immigrants and the Farmworkers Movement* (Seattle: University of Washington Press, 2000), pp. 39-48.

16. Bob Santos interview, September 12, 2008.

17. Tai Phan *Fred Basconcillo: A True Historical Figure* (Essay, Skyline College, South San Francisco, December 15, 2005).

6. Reunions and Recognitions

I am a part of all that I have met.

Alfred Lloyd Tennyson[1]

Whenever members of the Bridge Generation would get together, the question, "Why can't we all get together more often?" or its corollary, "Have you seen so and so?" would be inevitably raised. As the years went by, particularly as they became empty nesters and approached retirement, the urge to see old friends grew increasingly.

In Stockton on October 6-8, 1989, *The Filipino American Historical Reunion—Pilgrimage of the American Born Filipino*, provided the opportunity many had been hoping for. Sponsored by the Filipino American Historical Institute, the event was a fund raiser for a planned Stockton Filipino museum. Following a Friday night reception, the reunion moved into high gear on Saturday with historical exhibits during the day and a dinner banquet and dance in the evening. The reunion ended on Sunday with a festive picnic featuring entertainment and Filipino food. The three-day event drew over 400 persons, many from the Bridge Generation.

The Stockton reunion proved that the camaraderie among former youth club participants was alive and well. Friendships forged 30-40 years earlier continued to be genuine and meaningful—regardless of how much time had passed. Perhaps most important, it provided the impetus and resolve to organize a reunion focusing solely on Filipino youth clubs and athletic tournaments of the 1940-50s.

Under the inspired leadership of the former Terri Romero (Isleton LVM), General Chairperson, and Dixon Campos (San Francisco Mangos), Co-chair, the "Grand Reunion of Filipino American Athletic Clubs" was held on November 1-2, 1991 at the Marriott Hotel in the East Bay city of San Ramon, California.[2]

Friday activities consisted of a golf tournament and an evening reception. A tennis tournament provided the Saturday fare. Both days featured exhibits displaying memorabilia such as photographs, trophies, programs, team rosters, score sheets, jackets, and uniforms of the old youth clubs. A dinner banquet and awards dance with music by a nine-piece band playing nostalgic swing and jazz music concluded the festivities. In addition, as previously noted, the dinner speaker was author and historian Fred Cordova, the self-professed "sixth man" of the old Stockton Padres basketball team.

While not an official part of the reunion, the informal after-hours sessions in the hotel's spacious hospitality room on Friday and Saturday nights proved to be equally popular activities. There, singers and musicians took turns entertaining the Bridge Generation crowd with nostalgic songs and jazz tunes. The reunion included so many talented professional and amateur entertainers that hardly a minute passed by without someone performing at the microphone and piano. Among the musicians and singers were: Flip Nunez, Josie Canion, Rudy Tenio, Rosie Tecson, Corney and Connie Pasquil, Hamilton Burila, Primo Kim, Georgiana Leong, Victor and Sonja Gorre, Adele Urbiztondo, and Ted Reyes. For most of the evening a steady din of conversation, the clinking of glasses, and an occasional burst of laughter provided a nightclub-like atmosphere to the festivities. Whenever an old romantic ballad was sung, however, the hospitality room suddenly turned quiet, as the Bridge Generation crowd—many through misty eyes—reminisced of the bygone days of their youth.

The Grand Reunion was a resounding success. Attendance at the dinner banquet attracted a turn away crowd of more than 700 persons, capacity for the banquet room. Representatives of the old youth clubs attended in force. While most of the attendees were expected from California and the adjoining states of Washington, Nevada, and Arizona, the reunion committee was pleasantly surprised when there were also attendees from the states of Hawaii, Colorado, Texas, and New York and the foreign countries of Saudi Arabia, Australia, Guam, and the Philippines—a truly international turnout. The large turnout from near and far confirmed that former youth club members indeed were eager to renew past friendships. It was like old times during tournament days—except for the gray hair and added poundage. Long ago relationships were renewed. The reunion even launched several marriages: George Campos of San Francisco and Gilbertine Cabreana of Santa Maria; Nena Tevas Ventura of Monterey Park and Rudy Calica of San Jose, Ed Ventura of Sacramento and Beverly Daquioag of San Francisco.

The basic format of the 1991 San Ramon Grand Reunion, featuring athletic events, memorabilia, and a dinner/dance, were featured in subsequent reunions in San Jose (1994, 1998, 2001), Santa Maria (1996, 1998, 2003), a second one in San Ramon (1997), Stockton (2002, 2005), Sacramento (2007), and in the Southern California communities of City of Industry (1993, 2004), Buena Park (1996), and Lakewood (2006, 2008). In addition Vallejo, San Francisco, and Salinas celebrated their own youth club reunions during the 1990s.

A special effort was made during the second Grand Reunion at the San Ramon Marriott on September 26-27, 1997 to include the next generation so that they could experience first-hand the long lasting camaraderie of their parents.[3] Bridge Generation invitees were encouraged to invite their adult children, now in their 30s, 40s, and 50s to the reunion. Moreover, the banquet program carried out the two-generational theme with two emcees (Pete Jamero and Georgie Ente Leong) and two speakers (Joe San Felipe and Mona Pasquil) representing the Bridge Generation and the next generation, respectively. The response was gratifying, drawing more than 600 participants to the reunion. It was also heartwarming to watch the Bridge Generation and their adult children compete against one another in the tennis, bowling, and golf events and enjoy each other's company at the evening banquet.

Beginning with the 2006 Lakewood reunion and continuing with the 2007 reunion in Sacramento, the adult children of the Bridge Generation have assumed major responsibility for organizing the reunions as a tribute to their parents. The change was greeted with great relief by their senior citizen parents who continue to look forward to the reunions but who no longer have the necessary energy to put them on. A hoped for result of the next generation's efforts in organizing the reunions is that it will continue to build enduring relationships with their contemporaries from other communities similar to that enjoyed for the past 50-60 years by their parents.

The reunions have been precious opportunities for Bridge Generation Filipino Americans—now in their 60s, 70s, and 80s—to enjoy the lasting friendships forged from their youth, to relive the days of youth clubs, and to reconfirm their unique sub-culture.

Attendance has steadily decreased from highs of 600-700 persons during the early years to 250-400 of more recent years—not unexpected given the aging population of the Bridge Generation.

In 1994, the Filipino American National Historical Society (FANHS) devoted the entire program of its fifth national conference to the Bridge Generation.[4] Its theme—"Honoring the Bridge Generation: Sons and Daughters of Filipino Pioneers." The conference site of San Francisco was most appropriate to this celebration of second generation Filipinos. Within a 100 mile radius of San Francisco was estimated to be more members of the Bridge Generation than in any other part of the country. Most were formerly affiliated with the 30-40 youth clubs that flourished in the Northern California and the Central Valley during the 1940s-50s. Thus, it was not surprising that the conference attracted more than 500 persons—a FANHS record. There was another reason to celebrate— Ben Cayetano had just been elected as Governor of the State of Hawaii, the first Bridge Generation Filipino American to attain that prestigious position.

Workshops were grouped by the following tracks: Bridge Generation, How-To, Growing Up Brown, History, Research, and Young Adults. Among the workshop offerings at the two-day national conference were topics relating to campo life, mixed race, queen contests, youth clubs, and Filipino-Japanese Americans. The workshop on youth clubs, covering much of the experiences discussed in Chapter Three, drew strong interest from former club members eager to relive the halcyon days of their youth as did the workshop on mixed race in which panelists discussed their experiences of growing up Filipino with

Black, Japanese, Native American, Mexican, and Caucasian mixtures. Academic topics also proved to be popular. An overflow audience attended the workshop on the controversial Depression-era Filipino Federation of America with professors Steffi San Buenaventura of UCLA and Michael Cullinane of the University of Wisconsin sharing their research findings.

Perhaps the most emotional workshop was, "Filipino-Japanese Americans: In the Aftermath of World War II." Often fighting through tears, the panel members—born in America of Filipino fathers and Japanese mothers—recounted being rejected by Filipinos and other Americans. They described the fear and humiliation of being interred in relocation camps surrounded by barbed wire and armed guards. A non-interred member of the panel, Ted Munar from Santa Maria, California, moved to Arizona so that he could visit his interred Japanese mother regularly. Josephine Saito Espineda Paular of Stockton, spoke of the hurt she felt after hearing disparaging "Jap" remarks of her mother from hypocritical Filipina mothers, supposedly close friends, prior to the outbreak of the war.

General session presentations included "The Boogie Woogie Boys"—the First and Second Filipino Infantry Regiments of the U.S. Army—by San Francisco State University Professors Alex Fabros, Dan Gonzales, and Dan Begonia which attracted numerous Bridge Generation regiment veterans; an exhibition by the award-winning Filipino Youth Activities Drill Team of Seattle; an intergenerational panel discussion on politics with Sacramento Municipal Court Judge Tani Cantil, Daly City Councilman Mike Guingona, former Seattle City Councilmember Dolores Estigoy Sibonga, Peace Corps Associate Director Stan Suyat, HUD Secretary Northwest Representative Bob Santos, and former member of the Santa Barbara County Board of Supervisors Gloria Megino Ochoa.

A conference highlight was the presentation of the VIP (Very Important *Pinoys/Pinays*) Awards for lifetime achievement by Bridge Generation individuals at the Saturday night dinner banquet. Chosen by a panel of non-Filipino academicians from nominations submitted by FANHS chapters across the country, selection was based on the nominees' contributions to: (1) their field or profession and (2) the Filipino experience in America. A significant number of the achievers were former youth club members. Of the nineteen VIP Gold Awards, nine were ex-youth club members and five of the sixteen VIP Silver awardees, were formerly affiliated with youth clubs[5]—a clear reflection of the growing up value of youth clubs.

The dinner speaker was Fred Cordova—FANHS founding president, fellow Bridge Generation Filipino American, and former member of the Stockton "Padres" youth club. He paid tribute to the old youth clubs with poignant reminders of being a part of a different and happier past. And finally, to the loud and enthusiastic approval of his contemporaries, Cordova closed his remarks by once again bemoaning the lack of respect and recognition accorded to the Bridge Generation by mainstream America and by other Filipinos.

Notes

1. Alfred Lord Tennyson in Robert I. Fitzhenry ed. *Harper Book of Quotations* (Harper Collins Publishers, New York) 2005.

2. Official program, The Grand Reunion, Filipino American Athletic Clubs, 1940-1970s, San Ramon, CA, November 2, 1991.

3. Official program, Grand Reunion II of Filipino Americans, San Ramon, CA, September 26-27, 1997, p. 4.

4. Official program, Fifth National Conference, Filipino American National Historical Society, San Francisco, CA, August 3-6, 1994.

5. Very Important Pinoy/Pinay Booklet, Fifth National Conference, Filipino American National Historical Society, San Francisco, CA, August 3-6, 1994.

7. Ordinary Yet Extraordinary

What is remarkable is not how many failed in the face of discrimination, but rather how many men and women overcame the odds, how many were able to make a way out of no way for those like me who would come after them.

Barack Obama[1]

If there is a common characteristic among Bridge Generation Filipino Americans, it is one of quiet dedication and determination to live the life denied their immigrant parents.

The Filipino parents of the Bridge Generation—most of who were recruited by American agri-business to fill critical farm worker gaps during the 1920s-30s—came to the United States to live a better life. Like other immigrants, they simply wanted to "fit in" as Americans, to work at a job with a decent wage, and to be treated with respect—modest goals that were not always attained. While they may have been thwarted in reaching these goals, they looked to their Bridge Generation children to have better success. Their dutiful children went into American society with a strong commitment to live up to the expectations of their parents.

The following pages include the life stories of selected Bridge Generation Filipino Americans and are meant to put a human face on the experiences as described in previous pages. Their life stories reflect the quiet dedication and determination to live the life denied their immigrant parents. Their life stories also reflect their parents' modest hopes that their children would be able to "fit in"—not necessarily to be among the rich and famous, but, like most Americans, to be "ordinary yet extraordinary" in contributing to the greatness that is America.

Lastly, an explanatory note—the vast majority of Bridge Generation Filipino Americans grew up in California and participated in youth club tourneys and dances. Consequently, most of the following life stories are reflective of those experiences.

SAMUEL CATIEL GARCIA

"Growing Up in the Salad Bowl of America"

It was in 1948, following the establishment of the Livingston Filipino American Youth Club Dragons, when I first witnessed Sam Garcia's athletic prowess. At the time he was the mainstay of the Salinas Filipino Youth Council's basketball team—one of the few teams in the California youth club circuit that could effectively compete with the vaunted San Francisco Mangos. Not surprisingly, Salinas' game against the newly formed Dragons turned out to be a rout.

I would not personally meet Sam until the mid 1950s. He had long since retired from active play and, like most of his contemporaries, was busy providing for his young family. Through the years we have sustained our friendship through the various Filipino American old timer reunions and at family social functions. Now 82 years of age, Sam remains the same soft spoken and respectful person I knew as a young man. When I initially approached Sam about sharing his life story, he was hesitant. By a happy coincidence, however, his daughter, Jeanne Garcia Cordero, was in the process of researching their family history. She volunteered to help her father write his life story. The manuscript that resulted from their efforts provides the basis and inspiration for the following account of his life.

Born on September 8, 1926 in Wailua, Haleiwa, Oahu, Sam is the second son of Henry Demetria Garcia from the province of Negros Occidental and Felisa Saavedra Catiel from the tiny island of Siquijor. They were part of the great sakada immigration of the early 1900s that brought thousands of Filipinos from the Philippine regions of the Ilocos and Visayas to Hawaii to toil in the sugar plantations. Shortly after meeting one another in 1918, his parents were wed at the Catholic Mission in the capital city of Honolulu. Less than a year later, the family would settle in California's Salinas Valley—the Salad Bowl of America—which, except for the "Little Manila" city of Stockton, was the home of more Filipinos per capita than any other community on the American mainland.

During Sam's formative years, the family lived in Blanco, Buena Vista, and Four Crossing—small rural communities in the surrounding countryside—before settling within the city of Salinas. Over the years, his industrious and hard working father oversaw hundreds of young, mostly single, Filipino farm workers. At one point, he operated several farm labor camps simultaneously. He also farmed by leasing acreage and share-cropping. However, the early 1930s were the days of the Great Depression. Sam recalls:

> Whenever we moved, all of our family moved together, including uncles, aunts, and cousins when they were around. This was like any other ethnic group at

that time and promoted the feeling of acceptance. Back in those days, places weren't readily available. It was Depression time. A man . . . one of our workers . . . always brought home chicken. He got the chickens to feed the family. I assume he stole them. This was during the winter, there were no jobs. Farming was seasonal, so the family would go to the ocean to fish. We'd go to the Marina Beach and Moss Landing quite a bit. That's how we fed the family. . . . It seems like we ate a lot of fish and rice.

Sam's athletic skills were honed in the rural countryside. He remembers playing soccer, softball, hunting, and fishing. With the help of his father, he made his own stilts and played soccer on them, using a can for a ball. Sam believes that playing soccer on stilts helped with his coordination and agility—skills that would later serve him well on the basketball court. Coordination and agility also aided him in track and field. During his grammar school days, Sam and his older brother Jim competed as a two-person team in a track meet for all Salinas Valley schools sponsored by the YMCA. They finished in second place in overall team competition, taking first in the broad jump, the 50-yard dash, and the 100-yard dash.

Sam remembers his early years in the countryside as a constant adventure of good times. The only exception was when he was eight years of age during the height of the Great Depression.

> During Christmas the fire truck would come along and deliver gifts to the kids. The truck drove up and delivered gifts to our white neighbors. And I just stood there waiting for my turn. Then, they went right by me. I felt bad because I really wanted a toy. I didn't realize it at first. It was because I was different.

Typical of country schools at the time, several grades were taught in the same classroom since the number of students in each class was so few. "At Blanco School I earned the distinction of being the valedictorian of my graduating class," says Sam, quickly adding with a wink, "of course I was the only student in my class."

> In 1941 . . . I went to Salinas High School. For a few of the kids from Blanco, a high school with so many classrooms was too overwhelming and they never entered the school. I was fortunate enough to excel in sports and played volleyball, basketball, football, and track and lettered in them all. I was co-captain of our all-county basketball team. My Mom and Auntie would root me on at my football games, although my Auntie didn't quite understand the concept of tackling and would yell at the other players when I'd get tackled. In track I set the record for the 120-yard high hurdles in 14.9 (seconds). . . . It took 20 years until it was broken in 1964. . . . I was so involved in sports that I didn't pay attention too much to the social thing. Also because I did well in sports people accepted me and got to know me and like me.

These were also the years when Sam was involved with the Salinas Filipino Youth Council. He not only starred on its basketball team but also served as a role model for a steadily increasing number of Filipino youth.

While Sam's father influenced him through his traits of hard work, industriousness, and entrepreneurship, it was his mother who exposed him some to some of the finer things in life—such as music.

> Our family loved music. Mom had a beautiful voice and loved to sing. During the war the family played as an orchestra. Our cousins would come to stay with us in the summer.... Dorts played drums, Evie cello, David baritone sax, Al trumpet, Jim and I sax.... The girls played violin too. We played at the Oakland Civic Auditorium on Jose Rizal Day....We played for the Filipino Regiment at Camp Roberts.

Sadly, playing the saxophone also led to another incident of prejudice. Sam played in a local swing band that was preparing to play for a dance.

> A week before the event the band leader told me the owners of the place found out I was Filipino. The owner told him, we don't go to their dances and they should not come to ours.... I remember feeling "... you don't want me to play for you, (then) I don't want to play for you."

High school years were not all play, however. When Sam was thirteen he farmed with his father as he leased or sharecropped at the rate of 70:30 or 75:25. He also worked alongside the Filipino farm workers.

> I'd always work in the summers and when I could, after school. I'd be in the fields with the men by six a.m. We'd work all day until the field was finished, sometimes ten to twelve hours, when we were harvesting. When we tended the fields, hoeing the weeds we'd always work until dusk. It was hard work, stoop labor; topping beets, thinning lettuce. We'd make 25 cents an hour.

Sam enlisted in the Army Air Corps in 1944 but did not get called to active duty until 1945, shortly before the end of World War II. He learned to fly while stationed in Amarillo, Texas and later served at bases in Virginia and Clark Field in the Philippines. Being in the Philippines was fortuitous. He was able to surprise his older brother Jim—stationed at another military base—by attending his wedding.

> I think it was because of the war that I began considering myself an American Filipino. When I was in the service it was a way to clarify that I was a citizen. Not everyone was. In fact, when we came to Salinas in 1927, the overwhelming majority of Filipinos were "Nationals".

As far as Sam is concerned, he has two types of friends—Filipino friends and athletic friends. He still considers his family as his best friends. And while he rarely sees old athletic friends from his high school days, he has maintained contacts with long time Filipino American friends from the Filipino youth club days, largely through old timer reunions which Sam and his wife Aurelie have regularly attended since the reunions began in 1989. Seeing old friends at the reunions have proven to be meaningful to Sam and Aurilie. In 2007 they brought their children and their spouses to the reunion in Sacramento so they too could share the camaraderie their parents have long enjoyed with old friends.

In reflecting back on his life, Sam is thankful for his father's values of hard work and industriousness and his mother's love of music and love of people. "I think I got my sense of humor from her," says Sam. Most of all, he is thankful and proud of raising his seven children with Aurilie. "They are all individuals and I see the goodness in each of them."

MERCEDES ARRO CONCEPCION

"From America to the Philippines and Back"

As I approached Mercedes "Meding" Arro Concepcion's home, I was immediately struck by the beauty of its setting. The house is located in the hills of El Cerritto CA with sweeping views of the San Francisco Bay, the Golden Gate and Bay Bridges, and the skyscrapers of "The City" in the background. Her successful beauty shop, the Kensington Style House, is located nearby.

A Filipino Community beauty queen as a teenager, Meding is still strikingly attractive at 76 years of age. She has done well and is comfortable in her golden years. It was not always so.

Meding was born in 1932 in the small town of Gilroy, California—the "Garlic Capital of the World", the youngest of seven children of Eugenio Evangelista Arro of Cebu, Philippines and the former Timotea Banios of Dimao, Bohol Province. Her father died when Meding was only sixteen months old. Her mother married soon after and would go on to bear a total of seventeen children. Meding's family first immigrated to Hawaii during the mid 20s, among thousands of Filipinos from the Ilocos and Visayan regions of the Philippines recruited by the Hawaiian Sugar Planters Association. The family then moved to Davenport, CA, a tiny Central Coast community about thirty miles north of Santa Cruz, at the urging of relatives. Meding was born shortly thereafter.

When Meding was four years old, the family returned to the Philippines, taking advantage of a provision of the federal Filipino Repatriation Act of 1935. In actuality, the act was an anti-immigrant law that reclassified all Filipino immigrants as aliens from their previous status as Philippine nationals. It also provided for the return of Filipinos and their families to their native land but only on the condition that they not return to America. At the time, the country was still reeling from the Great Depression. Times were hard for the family. A return to the Philippines at no cost appeared to make sense. The plan was to go to Meding's mother's hometown in Bohol and start a *sari-sari* (Mom and Pop store) business. Unfortunately, the venture was a complete disaster—their chickens died of plague and their hogs drowned in a storm—the family lost everything.

The family then moved to Misamis Occidental Province on the northern coast of Mindanao only to be caught up with the onset of World War II. One of the first areas invaded by the Japanese, the province quickly became a hotbed of guerilla resistance. As Americans, the family was a prime target of the Japanese. The family spent the next five years on the run. Meding recalls:

> Sometimes we could hear the Japanese questioning neighbors next door, raping women, and killing people on the streets. We lived day by day, capturing loose chickens to eat,.and depending on the kindness of people.

Because there were guerillas who secretly mingled among the people, we were able to be warned ahead of time. We were lucky and were never caught. Before the outbreak of World War II, Meding's oldest brother, Phil, was drafted into the Philippine army. Because he was also an American citizen, he joined the U.S. Army at the end of hostilities in 1945 and returned to America. A younger brother, Bobby, was also able to return to the United States at about the same time. Upon their return, Phil and Bobby immediately found work on Davenport area farms. In a few years, they were able to pool their money and brought Meding and their sister Gloria back to America.

Meding remembers being so happy to be back to the land of her birth. School in Davenport was another matter. World War II had taken several years from her learning. She found herself repeating the third grade, losing several grades in the process. And since she left America when she was only four, she didn't know the English language. Meding had to learn English on her own, mostly by reading comic books. Batman, Superman, and Archie were some of her favorite comics. She knew the escapades of Batman and Robin and of Superman and his various nemeses by heart. She followed all of Archie's adventures with Betty and Veronica.

Her move to Isleton in 1949 was a godsend. Her uncle and benefactor, Pedro Evangelista, owned a combination grocery store and soda fountain, and gave Meding a part time job. This was not the only work for Meding. During weekends and vacations, she also worked in the fields and canneries picking and processing fruits and vegetables such as strawberries, cucumbers, pears, onions, tomatoes, asparagus, and peaches. And for Sunday *sabongs* (cockfights), she regularly made *biko* (sweetened rice) and fried chicken.

Meding was also adept at raising money. In 1950, she ran for queen in a statewide contest sponsored by the Legionnarios Del Trabajo, a Filipino fraternal organization. In order to win she had to sell the most tickets and participate in "social box" dances. She literally had to "run", since a tabulation dance was scheduled every weekend in cities and towns across California. In the end, she was awarded the top prize of Queen at the final tabulation in Stockton, winning over twenty other beautiful *pinays* (Filipinas).

Besides giving her spending money, her work at Uncle Pete's store was also an opportunity to improve her halting English and meet new friends. Most important, it was the first place since she left the Philippines where there were so many Filipinos. Rio Vista High School was also a decided improvement. There, she quickly bonded with other Bridge Generation *pinoys and pinays* who were pleased to have a new Filipina in their midst. From time to time, however, she felt the sting of discrimination from her white high school classmates and got into a few fights with girls. After one of her fights, a boy yelled, "I wouldn't even want to go out with someone like you."

The move to Isleton coincided with the Filipino youth club movement in California. Not to be outdone by the local boys who had established their own club team, the girls organized themselves into the LVM (Luzon, Visayas, Mindanao) Club. Meding was an original member of the club that later had the distinction of being the only girl's club to also host a boy's basketball tournament.

At the time, Isleton had the reputation among young Filipinos of having the most attractive girls. Thus, on weekends it was not unusual for many out of town guys to visit. Meeting many other young *pinoys and pinays* at the basketball and volleyball tournaments also served to increase the popularity of the Isleton girls. Meding soon found herself seeing more and more of Hansel Robles—a tall, handsome San Francisco Mango. She was nearing 21 of age and felt she should be married. To her disappointed, she learned that Hansel was only 18 and considered himself to be too young to get married.

Coincidentally, Isleton resident Danny Concepcion had just been discharged from the Army and asked Meding to accompany him to an ex-girl friend's wedding. Romance quickly bloomed. A year later they were married.

Uncle Pete had considered Danny to be "a good catch" and made sure that he was one of the first persons she met when she moved to Isleton. But Danny didn't seem to be interested in her at the time. Meding amusingly surmises, "He probably didn't like the way I spoke English." Danny was from a family of achievers. He graduated from the University of California at Berkeley with a Bachelor of Science degree and became a specialized medical technician. Within just a space of a few years Meding and Danny became parents to four children: David, Cindy, Ron, and Michael.

After the birth of Cindy, Meding went to cosmetology school at nights and quickly got a job to help support their growing family. The job was in a beauty shop in a posh little neighborhood—the Kensington Style Shop—just down the hill from her home. When the shop became available for sale, Meding bought it. She found she had a good head for business—learned after her years of working in Uncle Pete's store. The business thrived and continues to draw regular customers after forty-four years under Meding's ownership. Business was so good that it helped to send all four of their children to private school and to college.

Not surprisingly, Meding has no question about her ethnicity. She is still fluent in her native Cebuano dialect. Spending her early years during World War II in the Philippines and valuing the multi-cultural diversity here in America has only deepened her appreciation of being a Filipina American. According to Meding, however, her children are "Americanized". While they don't deny their ethnicity, they don't identify as strongly as she does on being Filipino.

In 2007 Meding celebrated her 75th birthday party at a private club in the foothill community of Moraga, California. It was a grand affair hosted by her children. Everyone was there—her children, grandchildren, siblings, relatives, and friends. Everyone that is except for her beloved Danny who passed away with cancer in 1992.

CORNELIO "CORNEY" PASQUIL, JR.

"The Filipino American Bill Evans"

I first met Corney in 1960. At the time he was playing piano with a jazz trio at the Berry Patch—a small, non-descript night club in the north end of Sacramento with sawdust for a floor. I've been a jazz aficionado since my teenage years. But my going to the Berry Patch that evening was not because of my love for jazz. Rather, my wife Terri and I were there to meet Corney. Our long time friend, Connie Viernes, had raved excitedly about this Filipino American from Kansas—of all places—who she recently met. She had seen him several times since and sounded like this might be a serious relationship. So serious, that Terri and I were concerned for Connie—skeptical that an unknown, itinerant Filipino piano player that just arrived in California might not be the right person for our close friend.

We needn't have worried. From the outset Corney impressed us as a quiet and respectful person. He clearly was a Bridge Generation Filipino American with many of the attitudes, mannerisms, and outlook of life of counterpart Californians. If we didn't know he was born and raised in Kansas, we would have assumed him to be from California. Most important, he was seriously smitten with Connie. Their ensuing courtship was brief—a veritable whirlwind courtship. Less than a year later they were wed at the local Catholic Church in Connie's picturesque Delta home town of Walnut Grove.

As to the opening reference to Bill Evans, he is my all-time favorite jazz pianist. For those who may not be familiar with my passion for straight-ahead jazz, Evans was perhaps the quintessential jazz pianist of the modern era who influenced most of today's pianists. He possessed an incomparable lyrical, yet swinging, playing style. I bought his every record, tape, and compact disc that I could get my hands on. In one of those strange coincidences, I had discovered Evans about the same time I met Corney. After seeing Evans in person in a San Francisco appearance a few years later, it suddenly dawned on me that Corney possessed the same lyrical style of jazz improvisation. He even was partial to Evans' tendency of hovering over the piano with his face just inches away from the keyboard. When I called the similarities to him, Corney's self-effacing response was to simply utter, "Really?"

Cornelio Pasquil Jr. was born in Fort Riley, Kansas on April 7, 1932, the son of a career army musician father and Simenona Rojas Pasquil. Originally a Philippine Scout, his father enlisted in the U.S. Army to join the 9th Cavalry—an all black unit then assigned to the Philippines. The only available slot in the army was with the 9th Cavalry. *Manong* Cornelio jumped at the chance to go to America as a soldier.

Although Corney's parents were both natives of the island of Cebu, Philippines, they met at Fort Riley for the very first time during the mid 1920s. At the time Corney's mother was visiting her sister, the wife of an African American soldier stationed there. Thus began a five year courtship, presumably the result of the couple's adherence to the traditional Filipino value of waiting for a proper time frame before marrying.

Corney quickly reminded me, "These were the days of segregation in the military; my father was one of the few Filipinos in the unit." Under the army's segregationist practices, Filipinos were limited to duty as cooks, butlers, housekeepers, or as in the case of Corney's father—musicians. Not surprisingly, the small Filipino contingent maintained close contact with one another. They were not the only Filipinos to visit. From time to time, Filipino hobos impacted by the Great Depression would leap from passing railway cars and find their way to the Pasquil home. As Corney listened in on the conversations of his parents during such visits from Filipino soldiers and hobos, he gained additional knowledge of the Filipino experience in America.

An ironic twist in race relations concerned the unit's black/Filipina couples. During the 9th Cavalry's tour of duty in the Philippines, many the soldiers in the all-black unit married Filipinas. Upon the unit's return to Fort Riley in Junction City, Kansas, their *pinay* wives found themselves shunned by black spouses of other African American soldiers. Consequently, Corney's recollection of the Pasquil family's social life at Fort Riley also consisted of visits with the ostracized Filipinas and their soldier husbands. He remembers, "Our home was often a 'social agency' for *pinays* seeking help with problems they experienced in adjusting to their new lives in America." Upon reflection, Corney believes this early experience in the Pasquil home "social agency" was an inspiration for his later choice to enter the profession of social work and to become meaningfully involved in the Filipino community.

As a schoolboy in Junction City, Corney underwent teasing and taunting from black youth from Fort Riley families. He described himself as a "loner" who was forced to pay extortion money to his taunters as a "way to keep peace." Later on as a teenager, he ran around with white friends, except for one African American youth from the fort. In high school, his social life was limited. Corney remembers his white friends being told by their parents, "Tell your dark friend to go home." Dates with white girls were rare and only conducted secretly.

Under these circumstances, it is not surprising that Corney became increasingly rebellious during his teens—years in which he described himself as "bad news." He often courted favors from out-of-town girls with costume jewelry that he passed off as real diamonds. He regularly frequented Junction City's pool halls. He began smoking and drinking. Among his friends, he was usually the one who went to bootleggers for liquor (Kansas was a dry state). Corney's parents were never aware of this rebellious side of their son, especially his mother who always regarded him as a "good boy."

Fortunately, music was a significant balancing force for Corney. Inspired by his musician father, he received formal training in classical music as a young boy (as did Bill Evans). At fifteen he began playing piano for social functions that paid him five dollars per event. At sixteen, he formed his own successful band from which he was able to make even more money. After completing high school Corney enlisted in the Air Force rather than wait to be drafted into the army. It was while he was stationed in Texas that he discovered jazz. During a weekend pass, he wandered into a jazz club and was immediately mesmerized by the revolutionary bop music that was being played. He soon began playing with small groups in the area and quickly learned the intricacies of jazz improvisation.

Following his honorable discharge from the Air Force, Corney attended Kansas State University. When his subsequent college degree did not immediately yield the hoped for results of a good job, however, he went back to playing with local groups. One day, a musician friend suggested, "Why don't you come to Sacramento, California with me where there are a lot more opportunities?" Sacramento indeed had work for itinerant musicians. Corney soon was playing regularly at such venues as the Iron Sandal and the Berry Patch—where he would meet Connie Viernes, his future wife.

Corney's marriage to Connie was the beginning of a more stable existence. He obtained a job as a social worker with the Sacramento County Department of Social Welfare, working with the old age assistance and unemployed parents programs. After only a few years at DSW, he won an educational leave of absence and earned a masters degree of social work from the University of Pennsylvania, among the most prestigious schools in the country. Corney is indebted to his graduate work at Penn for another reason. Although he grew up with Filipino values, he didn't always understand their genesis or purpose within Filipino culture. His research in writing many papers and essays while going through graduate training was invaluable in helping Corney better understand and become much more secure in his Filipino identity. Following his return to Sacramento County, his graduate degree proved to be of great help as he moved up the agency promotion ladder. He would work for DSW for the next twenty years, retiring as a division head.

Following his retirement from the county, Corney continued his part time employment at a non-profit children's agency, worked as a social work consultant, and taught at the Sacramento State University School of Social Work. Throughout his career, he never gave up his music—working periodically at local "gigs" as a soloist and with jazz groups. However, now that he is retired his "gigs" have steadily decreased.

Corney is understandably proud of the accomplishments in his professional career. It enabled him and Connie to raise five children and send them all to college and on to successful careers of their own. He and Connie still live in the large two-story home in the quaint Delta community of Walnut Grove just below the levee of the meandering Sacramento River. He is thankful for his many blessings, especially being a grandparent four times over. With a twinkle in his eyes Corney says, "My biggest accomplishment is being able to live as long as I have."

Corney has devoted much of his retirement years attempting to resurrect Stockton's Daguhoy Lodge of the Legionnarios Del Trabajo—a Filipino Masonic mutual help organization. During the heyday of the *Manong* Generation, the Daguhoy Lodge was a thriving center that hosted numerous activities for the Filipino community. Local Bridge Generation Filipino Americans still have fond memories of receiving Christmas presents as children during the Great Depression—grateful to the lodge for giving them the only presents they would get during America's worst economic downturn. At its peak, lodge membership was in the hundreds. With the demise of the older generation, however, membership dwindled considerably. Corney, with the considerable help of his wife Connie, has worked tirelessly to return the lodge and its paid-in-full, combination headquarters and apartment building to their former glory.

The great majority of Bridge Generation Filipinos have shied away from affiliating with Filipino Masonic organizations such as the Legionnarios Del Trabajo, Gran Oriente, and Caballeros Dimas Alang that enjoyed overwhelming popularity among the *Manong* Generation. Corney is a notable exception. When asked why he is now choosing to work on behalf of the Daguhoy Lodge, he simply says, "I have too much respect for what the LDT meant to the old *manongs* to not do it. I want to preserve their memories." Thanks to his efforts, the Daguhoy Lodge building is now one of the sites of the Little Manila Historical Preservation Authority in Stockton.

CLEMENTE JOSEPH SAN FELIPE[2]

"A Mango Forever"

In early 1950 I was home on leave and eager to attend my first Filipino basketball tournament since my enlistment in the U.S. Navy in 1948. I was particularly looking forward to get a first hand view of the vaunted San Francisco Mango Athletic Club team that had been running roughshod over its youth club competition for years. The tourney was held in the Kezar Pavilion, next to San Francisco's beautiful Golden Gate Park. It was there that I first met Joe San Felipe. While the meeting was brief, I could sense, even then, that Joe was intellectually as well as athletically gifted.

Joe and his wife, the former Michael Diane Wilensky, reside in a spacious house in South San Francisco on a bluff overlooking the bay—a house they have called home for 42 years and where they raised their four children. At 82 years of age, Joe still has the same athletic carriage of his old basketball days. The first thing he said after exchanging pleasantries was to say how pleased he was to learn that I was writing a book on our generation. "I get very upset whenever I run into people, especially other Filipinos, being completely unaware that we even exist." Joe bristled.

Joe was the first American born Filipino to pass the California State Bar and subsequently had a successful career as an attorney. Most of his career was spent with the California State Department of Corporations, rising to the position of Supervisory Counsel—the highest civil service level in state government. Not surprisingly, Joe did not want to talk for long about his career. Rather, he preferred to talk about his background, the halcyon days with the San Francisco Mango-Athletic Club, and the years serving his country.

Joe was born on December 4, 1925 in San Francisco to a mother from England and a Filipino father, Clemente San Felipe, from Rizal Province in the Philippines. His father came to the United States in 1922—a "work away" seaman who worked on steamships and freighters to earn passage to America. He ended up in San Francisco and found work at St. Francis Hospital as a pantry man.

There he met Elizabeth Pratt, a practical nurse whose family was originally from a well-to-do family in Nottingham, England. However, Joe's maternal grandmother married a Catholic man and was disowned by her Protestant family. So his grandparents immigrated to Canada when Elizabeth was a little girl. Joe's maternal grandfather fought and died in WWI. His grandmother remarried and the new family moved to San Francisco where Elizabeth ultimately met Joe's father.

Joe's early life was spent in the Fillmore District of the Western Addition—present day Japan Town. The oldest of six children, he was the only one born in a hospital, presumably because his parents were both hospital employees at the time. Joe described his family as poor with the children wearing hand-me-down clothing. This was during the Great Depression. His father worked odd jobs, mostly in kitchens, wherever he could find work. He also worked periodically for the Works Progress Administration (WPA), a massive federal program that put unemployed people to work on large construction projects.

His classmates at the Fillmore District school were predominantly Japanese, with one black and only one other Filipino besides him. Joe remembers the Japanese kids as clannish and found himself getting into fights with them frequently.

As Joe was walking with his siblings one day, their parish priest asked, "Why aren't you kids in parochial school?" When the priest learned the family could not afford it, the priest helped them get enrolled at Cathedral Presentation School at no cost. The school was mostly white with no blacks and only a few Filipinos. They were taught in combination classes. There, Joe did well as he listened, learned, and absorbed subjects taught to classes above his own. After Cathedral Presentation, he won a scholarship to nearby Sacred Heart High School but declined to attend when, on a visit, he witnessed a Brother spanking one of the students.

Attracting the best students in the city, Lowell High was a difficult school to enter in 1939, as it is today. However, Joe's grades were so good that he was quickly accepted. The student body numbered 3000 with two blacks, many Japanese kids and, one Filipino—Joe. He made the track team, played basketball, and continued to do well scholastically. His social life was another matter. Not only was he the lone Filipino in school but he stood out in his hand-me-down clothes and was the object of snickers. On one of his rare dates, a white girl told him the next day that she couldn't date him again because he was "different". Joe was lonely at Lowell—a loneliness that only diminished after he joined the Mangos, the Merchant Marines, and eventually the U.S.Army.

Joe was recruited by the Mangos in 1940 in their second year of existence, along with Felix Duag and Dixon and Eddie Campos—all of whom would become long time members of the youth club, especially on its basketball and softball teams. The Mangos were particularly successful in basketball and seemed to not only have the best athletes but also the tallest. "How did this come about?" I asked. Joe wasn't sure. "We had a lot of tall mestizos, like me," he says. "But we also had a lot of good sized 'full Filipinos.'" When the subject changed to softball, I reminded Joe that whenever the Mangos went to the Central Valley to play the Livingston Dragons it seemed that they usually wilted as a consequence of the hot sun and the strong pitching staff of the Dragons. Joe was not willing to concede the point, preferring to attribute the Mangos' wilting to "off-days."

A more important reason for being associated with the Mangos was that it was a chance to meet and socialize with youth in other communities. Joe amplifies, "It was nice to get together with other Filipino girls that we hadn't met previously."

The Mangos played an important role in Joe's decision to serve his country. On December 7, 1941, Pearl Harbor Day, the Mangos were playing in a basketball tournament in San Francisco. Among the spectators was Julian Calegos, an original Mango, on leave after being drafted into the Army. The game was suddenly cancelled with the announcement, "All those in uniform return to their base." The announcement was also a call for the Mangos as they began to join the armed forces as if on signal.

Along with several of his friends, Joe signed up with the U.S. Navy. His friends were accepted but Joe was rejected for naval service because of color-blindness. Undaunted, Joe joined the merchant marine. "If I couldn't serve on a ship with the Navy, I could do it with the merchant marine," he says. For the next few years, his ship was involved in the bloody battles for Guadalcanal, Saipan, New Guinea, and Guam in the South Pacific for which he received three battle stars.

By the time Joe left the merchant marine in 1944 he found that many of his friends were undergoing basic training with the newly formed First Filipino Regiment of the U.S. Army. The regiment was established in 1943 following a nationwide petition to Washington, D.C. to form an all-Filipino unit to aid with the effort to free the Philippines. He went to the draft board and requested immediate induction into the Army where color blindness was not an issue. He also requested to be assigned to the "First Fil" so that he could be reunited with his old Mango pals.

The reunification with old friends almost didn't happen. When Joe reported to Fort Ord the sergeant on duty asked, "What are you, kid?" To which Joe replied, "Are you asking for my racial descent? I'm Filipino and Spanish on my father's side and English, Irish, and Scotch on my mother's side." The grumpy sergeant said, "You're going to be a problem," as he checked "Filipino" on Joe's papers. Although wearing the three battle stars he earned with the Merchant Marine made Joe unpopular with some of the non-commissioned officers, Joe had an incident free experience for the remainder of his basic training with the First Filipino Regiment.

The officers of the First Filipino Regiment were all white. The overwhelming number in the regiment of 7000 Filipinos was originally from the Philippines. American born Filipinos comprised only a small fraction of the regiment. Due to their difficulties in understanding the broken English of Philippine born Filipinos, the white officers tended to be more comfortable in communicating with the American born Filipinos. Consequently, they first looked to American born

Filipinos in considering regimental promotions to corporals and sergeants. Bridge Generation Filipinos such as Joe rose quickly in rank. By the time he was 20, he was a platoon first sergeant.

The "First Fils" arrived in the Philippines as World War II was coming to an end. Much of their duty there consisted of providing security for convoys, excavating bodies of the Bataan Death March, and mopping-up operations looking for stray Japanese in the jungles. Joe finally was able to return home in 1946—a year after VJ Day. "I had a good experience in the Army," he says proudly. "If nothing else it gave me confidence."

Just before Joe was mustered out from active duty, he signed up with the Army Reserves after learning that most of his old Mango buddies had become reservists. The reserve unit essentially was an extension of the Mango youth club since twelve ex-Mangos would eventually sign up. Its basketball and softball teams were comprised almost exclusively of Bridge Generation Filipino Americans from the Mangos. Joe remained with the Army Reserves for thirty-nine years, rising to full colonel in 1978, and retiring in 1985.

Joe's first civilian job was with the Simmons Mattress company where he eventually rose to the position of Labor Relations Director, preparing for the job by going to City College of San Francisco at night when he was 29 years of age. He remained with the company for seventeen years. However, his most important achievement at the company was marrying the office secretary, Michael Diane Wilensky, in 1957. At first, Michael's family was dubious about the union but once her father, an army veteran, learned that Joe was a high ranking officer in the reserves, the resistance dissipated. The marriage is now into its 51st year, producing four children—all of whom rose to executive positions in the corporate world. Sadly, Joe and Michael lost their oldest son, Clemente Joseph San Felipe, to an aneurysm several years ago.

Since he was already engaged in quasi-legal work at the company, Joe developed a strong interest in pursuing law as a career. He enrolled in the law school at Golden Gate University, going to classes at night. In 1962 he had the distinction of being the first American born Filipino to pass the California State Bar and soon after joined the state's Department of Corporation as an attorney. He rose rapidly up the department ladder—from Senior Counselor and eventually to Supervising Counsel, jumping over other attorneys with more seniority in the process. Joe retired in 1992.

Joe was active in the Bay Area's Filipino community in his early years as attorney—helping to establish the Filipino Bar Association of Northern California and writing the by-laws for the Filipino American Political Association. Except for his involvement with old Mango friends, old timer Grand Reunions, and the Filipino American National Historical Society, he has chosen to be in the background of community affairs in recent years.

Joe's continued close associations with the Mangos, reunions, and FANHS reflects his lifelong strong identification as a Filipino. Joe's Filipino identification was undoubtedly shaped from his experiences with discrimination, such as his high school dating experience described above. As a paper boy he was told by a customer, "I only want my papers delivered by an American boy." And as reflected by his encounter with the army sergeant, Joe was never afraid to assert himself as a Filipino. Joe adds, "But I know many others who didn't." Finally, Joe attributes his identification as a Filipino to his father. "I am very proud of my dad," explains Joe of his ethnic identification. "He worked hard for his family and was proud of his roots."

GREGORY BAUTISTA BAMBO

"From Dishwasher to Jet Pilot"

I first met Gregg in 1991 at the Grand Reunion of Bridge Generation Filipinos in San Ramon, California. He competed in the golf and tennis events and danced the night away with his wife Marie. However, he spent most of his time reminiscing and reliving fond memories with old friends. Since then, he has been a regular at subsequent old timer reunions and at FANHS national conferences where, at just shy of six feet, Gregg stood above most of his contemporaries.

I was somewhat apprehensive about asking the quiet and soft-spoken Gregg if he would be willing to share his remarkable life experiences with me. To my relief, not only was he willing to share his life story but he was refreshingly forthcoming. In response to my comment that I would probably use artistic license in developing his life story, he quickly answered, "Your artistic license is free to roam."

At 73, the still youthful looking Gregg lives in Salt Lake City with his second wife, the former Marie Dufresne of St. Sauveur, Canada and former Canadian ski champion, "Female Athlete of the Year," and World Cup downhill race competitor. At Salt Lake City, he has found an ideal place to play golf and tennis, and to restore and collect classic cars—activities that he enjoys passionately. As a resident of Salt Lake City—predominantly white and Mormon—Greg may be the city's only Bridge Generation Filipino. However, it hasn't kept him from maintaining close contact with old friends. He is a frequent visitor to California and never fails to see pals in the Bay Area and in Salinas.

Salt Lake City is a far cry from his beginnings. Born on November 26, 1935 in Los Angeles from the union of a Filipino father, Gregorio Sr. from Morong, Rizal Province and a Caucasian mother, American Ruth Sellers, Gregg was the innocent victim of California's miscegenation law. During a custody battle when he was six months of age, an insensitive judge awarded custody to Gregg's father. What was the basis of the judge's decision? He felt that Gregg mostly resembled his father in appearance and color and thus should be awarded to Gregorio Sr.

As a consequence Gregg was raised by his father and three of his father's bachelor *compadres* (godfathers) from infancy until he was eight years of age. This family arrangement suddenly ended with the onset of World War II when the bachelor *compadres* were drafted into the U.S. Army. Although his father received a deferment from the draft as sole provider for Gregg, there was no one else to care for him while he was away at work. Consequently, for the next five years Gregg lived in a series of foster homes in Los Angeles' Watts, San Francisco, Guadalupe, and Salinas—all areas near his migrant father's place of employment. To Gregorio Sr.'s credit, he maintained frequent visits with his son. Gregg's voice cracked slightly as he reflected, "My father was always in contact with me—at least weekly."

As can already be surmised, Gregg identifies strongly as a Filipino. "Having been raised in an exclusively Filipino environment until I joined the Navy, even though I was a *mestizo*, I thought of myself racially as Filipino," he says. "My diet was mostly rice and fish, occasionally chicken and pork. Other than my time in Watts, all of my socializing was with young Filipinos."

Of all the places he lived, Salinas—"America's Salad Bowl"—was perhaps most significant in helping to shape Gregg's ethnic identity. There, he joined the Filipino American Youth Club of Sacred Heart, playing on its basketball team that competed in Filipino tournaments across central and northern California. Performing with the youth club team in various tournaments was also "where I formed some lifelong friendships that continue to this day," Gregg fondly remembers.

Gregg's career as a pilot in the U.S. Navy and with Western and Delta Airlines was featured by a series of fortuitous rapid rises through the ranks. It began shortly after graduation from high school in Salinas in 1953. A navy recruiter enticed Gregg with offers of having his own private bed, all the food he could eat, and a chance to see the world with a wage of $75 a month. Having lived in bunk houses with Filipino farm workers in various labor camps for much of his young life, it was all Gregg needed to hear. He readily agreed and became an enlisted man in the U.S. Navy.

Joining the military may have been pre-ordained. Gregg recalls, "My father loved this country. I remember during World War II him telling me that this was my country and someday I might have to fight or die for it. That kind of stuck and maybe why being in the military was comfortable for me."

Because he was of Filipino ancestry, Gregg soon found himself as a steward's mate doing domestic work in an admiral's mansion. Under the Navy's racist policy at the time, Filipinos were automatically assigned as steward's mates, providing for the personal needs of naval officers—making their beds, serving their food, and cleaning their living quarters. Gregg didn't mind since "this was the best job he ever had." He diligently went about doing his work, efficiently and effectively. Soon after, an astute officer in his division, recognizing Gregg's strong work ethic and potential for other duty, arranged for a transfer to the Navy's elite Electronic Technician School at Treasure Island, California.

Gregg was no stranger to hard work. His strong work ethic was formed early. He recalls, "When I was nine, I got my first job—as a dishwasher, standing on a stool over a large basin with dishes stacked higher than I was tall." This was followed by a short stint as a pin setter in a bowling alley when pins had to be positioned by hand. The job soon ended when Gregg decided, "Drunk bowlers and hurtling bowling balls was a dangerous way to earn 10 cents a line." A job as a prep boy in an auto body shop, which formed the basis for his later passion for restoring classic cars, soon followed. When he was a high school student in Salinas, Gregg worked seven evenings a week at 75 cents an hour as a gas station mechanic and attendant. He worked double duty during weekends and school vacations, dry packing lettuce with Filipino farm workers in nearby fields during the day and working at the gas station at night.

In the mid-50s, the Navy came under public and congressional pressure to integrate its officer corps. Other branches of the armed services had already been integrated in accordance with President Harry Truman's 1948 Executive Order. As part of the Navy's program of compliance, Gregg soon found himself with the Naval Aviation Cadet Program in 1956. He was on his way to becoming a naval officer. He was commissioned as an ensign and received his naval aviator's wings in 1957—the U.S. Navy's first Filipino American naval aviator.

Gregg's first two duty assignments as a naval officer were ashore—as tactical officer with an anti-submarine warfare squadron and then for two years as a flight instructor and materiel officer for a combat fleet replacement squadron at Coronado, California during which time he was promoted to Lieutenant. His first shipboard duty came in 1963 on the aircraft carrier, the USS Midway. While at sea he was notified of his accelerated promotion to Lieutenant Commander, leapfrogging over 1,000 competitors that included Naval Academy graduates and officers who had seniority in years of service. At 28 years of age, Gregg was the youngest Lieutenant Commander in the entire U.S. Navy. "Not bad for someone who only had a high school education." he says proudly.

A fighter pilot while aboard the USS Midway, Gregg saw extensive combat during the Vietnam War. In recognition of his "shiphandling of an aircraft carrier and multi-ship task force maneuvering performance in a combat environment," he was awarded the Department of the Navy Achievement Award.

In 1965 Gregg transitioned from fighter pilot to fly the Douglas A3 "Skywarrior" bomber, the Navy's largest carrier-based combat plane. He was aboard the USS Forrestal in 1965 as a "Skywarrior" pilot and squadron commander during the Forrestal's tragic Vietnam deployment when 133 lives and 52 aircraft were lost.

Gregg flew numerous missions during the Vietnam War, sometimes having to land his damaged jet plane. One night, Gregg narrowly escaped disaster. As he attempted to make an emergency landing, he lost his last remaining engine. Fortunately, he was able to land safely—the only pilot to ever "dead stick" a "Skywarrior" to a safe landing on an aircraft carrier.

In 1968 Gregg was promoted to full Commander (complete with the coveted "scrambled eggs" on the bill of his cap). Shortly after becoming Commander, he resigned from active duty and went into the Naval Reserve, enabling him to accept a position as a pilot with Western Airlines—the first Filipino American pilot for a major airline.

Gregg's return to civilian life did not last long. In recognition of his impressive record and combat flight experience, the Navy recalled him to active duty to become commanding officer of the Naval Reserve's first A3 "Skywarrior" Squadron. At the age of 33, he was the youngest commanding officer of a combat squadron in the U.S. Navy. For the next seven years Gregg remained on active duty, getting yet another promotion—this time to the rank of Captain. He retired from the Navy in 1975 and returned to his old civilian job with Western Airlines.

Western Airlines merged into Delta Airlines in 1988. Gregg's career with the airlines was to last for twenty years, as he piloted and commanded a series of Boeing aircraft coast to coast, from Mexico to Alaska and up to Canada. In his career, he accumulated over 24,000 hours of flight time—the equivalent of eight years in the sky. Most impressive, however, was his record of flying over nine million miles for Western/Delta Airlines without a single incident. Retired since 1995, Gregg's flying days are not over as he makes regular flights to see his two sons—Gregg III in San Francisco and Bradd in New York City.

As noted earlier, Gregg's career in the Navy and with Western/Delta Airlines was achieved without the benefit of a college education. Gregg attributes his success to the inspiration and lessons learned from his father, Gregorio Sr. "My motivation in life was to make him proud of his son." said Gregg. He described his father as "extremely intelligent, who spoke three languages and several Filipino dialects"—despite lacking formal education. With a strong work ethic who always "took any work that was offered," Gregorio Sr. was Gregg's perfect role model. Among his father's jobs was motorcycle delivery boy, houseboy, caregiver, chauffer, apartment building superintendent, nightclub bartender, cook, chef with the Brown Derby in Hollywood, shipyard painter, automobile body and paint shop co-owner, carpenter, and migrant field laborer. Finally, true to his Filipino roots, Gregorio Sr. was also a skilled trainer of fighting roosters—a *sabongero*.

Gregg went on to describe his father as "an industrious and gentle man with high morals whom everyone trusted and loved. I admired those traits and tried to emulate them. He always was kissing me and telling me how much he loved me, even after I became an adult."

Gregg's personal philosophy is also attributed to his father: "Be proud of your heritage and do your best. Be positive and good things will happen." To that philosophy, Gregg adds his own: "Your friends are precious. Don't forget them."

SAMUEL CECIL AND NINA DUBLIN GONZALEZ

"Opposites Attract"

Following their respective retirements, Sam and Nina purchased a beautiful two story home in a brand new subdivision of Turlock, California—a Central Valley community that continues to undergo dramatic change. For years Turlock was mostly known for its many dairies and as the home of Swedish and other Scandinavian immigrants. The opening of California State University Stanislaus in 1960 began the change in its demographics. In more recent years Turlock has become the home of countless Bay Area commuters, attracted by its more affordable homes.

Sam had a successful career in art design. After getting his start with a Cleveland, Ohio greeting card company, he formed his own design company in

San Francisco (Top Drawer Studios) and went on to serve as art director for the *Modesto Bee* (California), a daily newspaper, for nineteen years before retiring in 1997. He also found time to volunteer for his community as an officer and member of the Board of Directors, United Way of Stanislaus County.

Sam has been consistently involved in Bridge Generation activities for all years that I've known him. Sam, along with Nina, was a regular participant at basketball and volleyball tournaments during the heyday of the youth club movement. In more recent years, they have attended all the old timer Grand Reunions as well. Sam was President of FACT (Filipino Action Coalition Today) for the ten year period 1971-81 and was the first Vice President of the Central Valley Chapter of FANHS (Filipino American National Historical Society) upon its establishment in 1998.

Thus, imagine my great surprise when Sam told me that has been the full extent of his association with other Bridge Generation Filipinos. As a youth, he spent most of his life with his father, the *manong* friends of his fathers, or with non-Filipinos—rarely with Filipino Americans his own age.

Samuel Cecil Gonzalez, Jr. was born on December 2, 1938 in San Francisco, the only child of Samuel Sr. of Bicol Province in the Philippines and Isabel Wightman, a Caucasian co-worker of his father. At the time both were employed at the posh Saratoga Inn, near San Jose, where his father was the chef. Reportedly, his birth "came as a surprise" to his unmarried parents. He never knew his mother as she left the family after only a few months. Inexplicably, his father was forced to legally adopt Sam even though there was never a question that he was the biological father.

Fifty years—roughly two generations—separate Sam and his father. With such a long span of time, one would not expect a close relationship to develop. Regardless, Sam attributes whatever success he may have achieved in life to the love he received from his father. "His love for me was never in doubt," said Sam, adding, "He told me every chance he could that he loved me."

The life Sam and his father led did not make it easy for their relationship to thrive. For five years, from the age of seven, Sam was boarded out to various families during the school year. Sam describes his father as "never having a problem getting a job at resorts and country clubs—he had a problem in maintaining a job."

As chef, Sam's father insisted on having his own crew of Filipino cooks, a significant factor in customer satisfaction—which is believed to be the reason why he never seemed to have a problem finding another job. Ironically, this same penchant for independent action inevitably led to conflicts with management and the need to find yet another position.

Sam Sr.'s independence originated at an early age. At thirteen, he ran away from his home in Bicol to escape a grandmother who "was losing her senses." In 1901 when he was fifteen, he worked as a steward aboard sailing ships. Four years later his father landed in San Francisco, a city still suffering from the devastation of the great earthquake of 1906. With the exception of a short period of time when he owned and operated a charter boat business in Alaska, the San Francisco Bay Area was where his father made his home.

With his father's every job change, Sam found himself in a different town, in yet a different living arrangement—San Francisco, San Mateo, San Luis Obispo, Vallejo, Riverbank and other forgettable communities. While most of the families with whom Sam was placed were white, two were with Filipino families. The first Filipino placement turned out to be traumatic for Sam when the family refused to give him back to his father because of the alleged non-payment for Sam's care. The placement with the family in Riverbank when he was twelve was much healthier. The family enjoyed warm, loving, relationships with one another. Moreover, the several children around the same age as Sam gave him needed companionship. Perhaps most important, it was a rare opportunity for Sam to experience traditional Filipino culture in a family setting. Riverbank's only downside was at the local grade school where, as one of the few Filipinos, he had to run a daily gauntlet of mostly Hispanic boys.

Sam looked forward to the summers when he was able to rejoin his father. Usually, they lived with other *manongs* in boarding houses. It was a womanless existence except for the times when "ladies of the night" would drop by. It was also an existence without other Filipino kids. To this day, Sam wishes he had an older brother.

When Sam turned twelve he was old enough to stay full time with his father, a time that he describes as "the happiest years of my life." His living arrangements were also a decided improvement. In the interim, his father had come back to work at the Saratoga Inn where the owner provided them with a three room apartment in which to live. Again, his father seemed to get his own way with the owner. Not only were the Filipino cooks handpicked by him, he also insisted on the hiring of more Filipino gardeners at the Inn.

Grateful for the opportunity to stay in one school, Sam took full advantage of his years at Los Gatos High School, where he made the swimming team. After graduation, Sam enrolled at San Jose State University. His father had saved enough money to pay for his entire college education. However, it was all gone by the end of the first year. According to Sam the money mostly went for "parties and girls". Chastened by his immature behavior, Sam enlisted in the Air Force.

Following his discharge, Sam returned to San Jose State University—wiser and more mature. There, he met fellow art majors, Ben Gonzales (no relation) and Primo Villarruz. Both were affiliated with Filipino youth clubs—Ben with United Filipino Youth of Stockton and Primo with the San Jose Agenda. Both were also well known to other Bridge Generation Filipinos on campus and in the San Jose community. In no time at all, Sam's circle of Filipino American friends grew rapidly.

In 1961, the San Jose Agenda hosted a sixteen-team basketball tournament that culminated with the customary awards dance in the evening. Sam didn't need much convincing from Ben and Primo to attend. At the dance, he noticed a slim, attractive *pinay* with an infectious smile who seemed to always be surrounded by a crowd of admirers. After learning from Ben that her name was Nina, Sam asked to be introduced. But by the time Ben got around to introducing them, it was almost midnight. Luckily for Sam who was not an accomplished dancer, the band was playing a slow tune when he asked Nina for a dance. It was love at first sight.

"It really was love at first sight," agrees Nina, adding with her ever present smile, "even though Sam didn't dance very well." Five months later, Sam asked Nina's mother and stepfather for her hand in marriage. Concerned that Nina was already twenty one and still not married, her parents and many aunts expressed a collective sigh of relief upon Sam's proposal. On March 31, 1962, Sam and Nina were wed—less than a year after they first met.

Born on January 3, 1941 in Stockton to a *manong* generation father and a Bridge Generation mother, Nina lived most of her formative years in Irwin, California, a small town about six miles from Turlock. As the eldest girl of a family of eight children, her early years were spent in helping her mother care for her siblings and learning how to cook while her parents worked in the fields.

Nina began going to youth club tournaments at the young age of twelve. She soon was playing girl's basketball and volleyball for the Livingston Filipino American Youth Association Dragonettes. With Nina, the Dragonettes won several big tournaments in the youth club circuit before age and motherhood took their toll.

Nina enjoyed her years in high school, participating in extracurricular activities and making many friends at the predominantly white school. When it came to boyfriends Nina drew the line. Her mother had always discouraged her from getting serious with *puti* (white) boys, preferring her to go with Filipinos. Since Nina was now a regular participant in Filipino American youth club tournaments and its award dances, however, she never had a problem in attracting admirers—much to the relief of her mother. One relationship did become serious. It only ended when the young man asked her to accompany him to college at Utah where he had just won an athletic scholarship. She refused. "I thought it was too much like shacking up," says Nina.

While Nina is well aware of historical discrimination against Filipinos and has prepared their two daughters—Shelley and Celeste—to deal with it, her personal experiences with overt discrimination have been rare. She attributes this to a change in how American society expresses prejudice. She explains, "During the days of my parents and older Bridge Generation Filipinos, discrimination was expressed in obvious ways. In more recent years, it is much more subtle." Regarding her years of living in white suburbia, for example, Nina always felt she was a "token brown" even though she never experienced an outward incident of discrimination. She has experienced many more instances of gender discrimination. Recently, when inquiring about purchasing a car for her own personal use, the car salesman turned to Sam to discuss the matter—ignoring Nina completely.

Nina worked for many years as an analyst at nearby California State University Stanislaus before her retirement in 1998. Periodically, the university calls her back on a temporary basis—a welcome change from retirement. Otherwise, she and Sam stay busy with their two daughters and three grandchildren, golf, and keeping in touch with her large extended family—which now numbers more than a hundred.

It is hard to imagine two people more unlike in temperament and background than Sam and Nina. Sam is basically shy while Nina is outgoing and friendly. Nina is from a large family of eight children; Sam is an only child. Sam moved around a great deal; Nina lived most of her life in communities within a thirty mile area. Nina was around young Filipinos all her life, whereas Sam's first association with the Bridge Generation dates back only to 1961. Their marriage, now into its forty-sixth year, has obviously worked. As the old saying goes, "Opposites attract."

JOSEPHINE SAITO ESPINEDA PAULAR

"A Proud Filipino Japanese American"

Throughout the many years that I've known Josie, she has consistently been the same quiet, unassuming, somewhat shy teenager that I met five decades ago. She speaks of her successful career as an educator only when asked. Outwardly, Josie demonstrates the personal satisfaction of being in a long and happy marriage and of raising two daughters to become independent women. Underneath that quiet demeanor, however, also lie disquieting memories that haunt her to this very day.

Josie was born on February 20, 1932 in Pescadero, California, a small Northern California town—equidistant from San Francisco and Santa Cruz—only a few miles inland from the Pacific Ocean. She was the youngest daughter of Simeon Espineda of Bicol Province in the Philippines and Tsuru Saito, born of Japanese ancestry on the island of Oahu, Territory of Hawaii. Ostracized by other Japanese for marrying a Filipino man, her mother put her energies into learning Filipino culture—eventually speaking several Filipino dialects as fluently as her Philippine-born relatives and friends.

When Josie was only a year old, her father passed away. Her mother's subsequent marriage to Jose Panoncialman of Carcar, Cebu resulted in the family moving to Stockton where her stepfather was a labor contractor. Her stepfather is the only father Josie has ever known. She regards him as such and is thankful for the support, care, and love he provided the family. In later years, Josie was to become especially grateful to him when he surprised her by saving enough money to enable her to complete her studies at the College of Pacific.

Josie has only a hazy recollection of her years in asparagus camps but recalls she "was the only female besides her mother—surrounded by many *manongs*." She was also literally surrounded by *manongs* at the Filipino Federation of America compound in which her family resided during her formative years. The compound, which still stands, consisted of a main hall in the center surrounded by housing for families and single men.

> I grew up in Stockton living on the grounds of the Filipino Federation of America. I grew up living the teachings of this organization. One of the things we were taught is our body is our temple and diet and exercise was very important.

The Federation, led by its charismatic founder, Hilario Moncado, believed that fasting and abstinence would protect them from life's temptations. Clean living was paramount. Alcohol and drugs was prohibited. Members were also taught to avoid eating meat. The organization drew most of its membership support from former sakadas (immigrants recruited to work on Hawaiian sugar plantations) from the Visayan islands of Bohol, Siquijor, Leyte, Negros, and Cebu—the birthplace of its leader. A lifelong member of the Federation, Josie grew up with the basic teaching of Moncado. Her early life was spent largely with Federation members and their families. Other Filipinos considered the Federation as clannish. But to Josie the members' preference for associating with one another was their way of maintaining the Federation's belief systems. To this day, the teachings of clean living continue to be of great significance for her.

Due perhaps to being the youngest daughter in the family, Josie enjoyed a close relationship with her mother. Reportedly, she has much of her mother's looks, temperament, and mannerisms. Thus, the forced evacuation and relocation of all persons of Japanese ancestry in the immediate aftermath of World War II was particularly hurtful for Josie, then ten years of age. She painfully remembers being pulled out of school and forced to sleep in the horse barns of the San Joaquin County Fairgrounds.

> Separation from family and friends was very traumatic. Everyone who had a drop of Japanese blood were asked to relocate. My mother, siblings, and I were made to leave our home and stepfather. Being herded and housed at the Stockton Fairgrounds surrounded by barbed wire fence and watch towers with guards ready to fire their rifles, I knew at my young age that this was wrong. Having friends who turned their backs to my mother because they thought she was the enemy was so hurtful and made her grow older before her time. My older brother joined the 442nd Battalion (the famed Japanese American unit—the most decorated of WWII) to prove that he was a loyal American and came home with a wounded arm that was a constant reminder of the casualties of war. Time should heal but we never forget.

After six months of enduring the squalid housing of the Fairgrounds, the government relocation authority relaxed their rules and permitted those of mixed heritage/marriage to return home. Josie and her family were finally able to go home.

Josie identifies herself as a Filipina American, not surprising given that her life experiences have been entirely in a Filipino cultural setting. At the same time she is proud of the Japanese heritage she inherits from her mother, regardless of the inhumane treatment that Josie and her family underwent during World War II.

Like everyone else following the end of the war, Josie concentrated on pursuing a course of normalcy. She was an exemplary student at St. Mary's High School, Delta College, and the College of Pacific where she received a B.A. in education. Thus began a thirty-three year career as an educator, first as a classroom teacher of primary grades and ending in teaching special education students. Josie worked in six different school districts and had the distinction of being the first Filipina American teacher in four of them—the Sacramento, Tracy, Whittier, and Upland Unified School Districts.

Josie acknowledges that she "developed late." She was not interested in boys as a teen and did not date until she was 24 years of age. Even her courtship by her husband of fifty years, Ray Paular, was somewhat delayed. It seems that when Ray first came to call on her, Josie, a devout Catholic, "gave him up for Lent." Ever persistent, however, Ray continued to court her, wearing his best clothes to impress not only Josie but also her parents who were wary of Ray who was divorced (true) and rumored to have several children (false). On their dates, her parents directed Ray to have her home by 9 p.m. Her parents actually preferred another young man for Josie. Upon learning this, Ray went to his rival telling him, "She loves me," which convinced his rival to stop pursuing her. Josie and Ray were finally wed on August 31, 1968 in a beautiful wedding on the campus of the University of Pacific with a large number of relatives and friends in attendance. Fifty years later, they celebrated their golden wedding anniversary on the same date and place, with many of the same guests in attendance.

Without hesitation, Josie considers that her greatest achievement in life is motherhood and "having two daughters who are drug free and contributors to our society." To which I would add "and being proud as a Filipina American and of my Japanese heritage."

FRAN ALAYU WOMACK

"Neighbor of the President"

I first met Fran, along with her older sisters, Terry and Ethel, at the very first conference of the Filipino American National Historical Society (FANHS) in 1987 in Seattle, Washington. Their presence, along with a number of other Midwest and East Coast attendees, provided a needed national atmosphere to FANHS, just in its initial phase of organization. Fran has attended all subsequent national conferences—held biannually—including the 2008 conference in Anchorage, Alaska, where she was elected national treasurer.

Since the distance from California to Chicago precluded a personal interview, Fran readily agreed to write her life story. The following account of her life, with minor exceptions, is essentially in her own words.

Fran was born in 1931 in Chicago, Illinois with the given name of Frances Belle Alayu. "The name doesn't even sound like me," says Fran. She is the youngest of three daughters of Francisco Paco Alayu and Melchora Gadduang Alayu—both from the municipality of Solano, Nueva Vizcaya, in the Philippines where they wed in 1919. Shortly after their marriage, her father immigrated to the United States, stopping for a year to pick apples in Sunnyside, Washington before going on to Chicago. While at Sunnyside, he also received his high school diploma. Her mother, nicknamed "Olang," remained behind to finish her studies at the Philippine Normal School in Manila. She subsequently taught for several years in her hometown of Solano as part of her contract to attend PNS.

Olang rejoined her husband in 1924 in Chicago where he had obtained employment at the University of Chicago Library. At the time, Fran's father was sharing an apartment with relatives and other town mates as was the custom of Filipino immigrants. "This situation was not to Mom's liking," says Fran. However, while participating in a campus program, Olang met a woman who was willing to rent a nearby apartment to the family. "There was always at least one uncle living with us, but my mother tolerated it because it was her apartment...besides, Filipinos take care of their relatives." The uncles were the girls' surrogate *lolos* (grandfathers). They helped with household extras and provided money for movies for the girls. Fran remembers, "You could always tell when they had a good tip day, won at the race track or at poker, because it meant dinner at Chinatown—sweet and sour pork, chicken chow mein, and egg foo young. I didn't know then that we were just the other side of poor during those post depression days."

The family settled in Hyde Park, home of the University of Chicago. Even then Hyde Park was an integrated neighborhood—one of the few in otherwise segregated Chicago. Fran still resides there. Hyde Park is also the neighborhood where Barack Obama has his family home. Since being elected President of the United States in 2008, of course, his residence has been at the White House in Washington, D.C.

During Fran's growing up years in Hyde Park, several families from the Alayu's home province of Nueva Vizcaya and its neighboring provinces of La Union and Pangasinan also settled there. She recalls, "The block where we grew up had about five families living in three apartment buildings, and there were two other buildings in the neighborhood with several Filipino families. There was comfort in numbers, and that made for a lot of neighborhood parties."

Fran remembers, "Mom and Dad made sure we were Americanized.... It began with enrolling each of us at the Hyde Park Baptist Church nursery school, where the mothers were invited to tea and the students helped make cookies and popped corn in the fireplace." Later, her mother became a Girl Scout leader and was active in PTA meetings and fundraisers. Her mother was also resourceful. She found a Jewish sponsored summer camp for the girls to attend at little expense. Fran and her sisters also went to outings such as the rodeo, the zoo, and the circus. To save money, her mother made sandwiches for the girls rather than having them buy expensive hotdogs or sandwiches.

The girls were also exposed to culture with trips for free concerts at the Grant Park Band Shell to hear Lily Pons and Caruso. Comments Fran, "You have to be more than three-quarters of a century old to know them. And of course, there were the piano lessons and also piano lessons, for me."

Summer vacations were spent with other Filipino families in Williams Bay, Wisconsin, sharing a cottage. Later the families would camp, tent and all, at the Indiana Sand Dunes. Fran surmises, "Since we didn't have a community or neighborhood, maybe that was why (Filipino) families were very close."

"Always on Sunday" is how Fran describes her Filipino acculturation process. Sunday included church services at the Filipino Community Center and lessons about the Philippines. During the summer, Sunday was when everyone attended the Philippine provincial picnics and softball games in Grant Park. In between were birthday parties, christenings, and the Philippine Women's Club meetings. Fran remembers, "These meetings always ended up in a recital. I firmly believe that anytime two or more Filipino families get together, it becomes a recital. Also, looking back, I think every family had a piano."

Fran remembers Filipinos to be "the only ethnic group that took their very young children to the many inaugural dances and Rizal Day banquets . . . other groups would leave their children at home with a sitter or other family members, but Filipinos do everything as a family, and, besides, the family sitter was also at the dances."

As a pre-teen, Fran was part of a dance group with other young Filipino Americans that performed at such venues as Soldier Field, particularly during World War II when being Filipino was popular. And like the "Always on Sunday" Philippine history lessons, the dance group learned about Philippine languages, dialects, and natural resources between performances.

Because Fran's family lived in the same apartment for many years, she grew up with the same classmates. As a result, she believes she was insulated from discrimination—until high school when she was nominated for prom queen. The nomination was not welcomed by some of her fellow students. Despite support from her English teacher and other students, Fran came in second in the selection for prom queen. However, she more than made up for that disappointment by becoming the first non-white cheerleader at Hyde Park High School and cheerleader captain during her senior year.

Fran was active in the civil rights movement during the 1960s and believes she may have been the only Filipino activist in Chicago at the time. She says this was "when Filipinos thought being brown meant you were almost white, but at least not black. This led to my involvement in politics, working for State Senator Richard Newhouse and the first Black Mayor of Chicago, Harold Washington." From those experiences, Fran went on to become Executive Director of the National Association of Minority Contractors in Washington, D.C. where she was involved in helping in the implementation of the controversial Minority/Women's Business Enterprise program. Ironically, although Fran married an African American man, he was not supportive of her involvement in the civil rights movement, describing him as subscribing to "the pull yourself up by your boot straps philosophy."

In addition to the "Filipino Firsts" that she achieved in high school, Fran is proud of the Fellowship she received to attend the Department of Urban Studies and Planning at the prestigious Massachusetts Institute of Technology in Boston. However, she is most proud of how her three children turned out. According to Fran, they all "have a sense of their Filipinoness" and continue to be influenced by lessons learned from their Filipino grandparents.

The children were also greatly influenced by Fran's strong identification as a Filipino American. Says Fran, "Because my folks instilled Filipino customs in us and our involvement in Filipino community activities, I grew up Filipino. Actually, the first time I was described as American was my first trip to Europe. And I am always American when I'm in the Philippines and every place outside the United States. It wasn't until the 'hyphen' became popular, did I, when asked, describe myself as Filipino-American." She doesn't know if considering herself as a Filipino American was the beginning of her involvement with FANHS. Be what it may, it was a meaningful revelation. To this day, she continues to be an effective spokesperson for the Filipino American experience—particularly from a Midwest perspective.

JOSE VALENTINO ORIARTE

"A Free Spirit"

As long as I can remember, Joe Oriarte has been a fixture at Bridge Generation events. During the heyday of the Filipino youth club movement, he was a perennial All-Star on the basketball court. In more recent years, he has been in attendance at virtually all the old timer reunions. I first met Joe in the late '40s when he played for the Vallejo Filipino Youth Recreation Association basketball team with his brothers, George and Burt, and future Santa Clara University star Eddie Chavez. Friendly, gregarious, and good looking, Joe seemed to know everyone and was popular among guys and girls alike. He also seemed to be always wearing a perpetual, infectious, and *maldito* (mischievous) smile. More than fifty years later, that smile is still there.

Arrangements were made to interview Joe at his San Leandro condo in June 2008. When I commented on the condo's clean and immaculate appearance Joe, a widower, replied, "Being neat and clean is something I learned long ago from my father."

It seems Joe's father, Guillermo Oriarte, was an influence from the time of Joe's birth in 1926 in Vallejo. It was his father who gave Joe the middle name of "Valentino" after Rudolph Valentino, the "Latin Lover" star of silent movies during the 1920s. Choosing "Valentino" for his son's middle name was also a clue to his father's personality. "He was a womanizer," says a smiling Joe. His father was also a good dancer, prompting Joe to add, "I'm just like my father."

Joe is from a family of five children—one girl and four boys. However, his growing up years was mostly spent with youngest brother Burt since the older siblings were living on their own. I was surprised to learn that Joe has a fraternal twin brother, Pedro, who he has not seen since the early 1930s. During those days, it was not uncommon for Filipino families with many children to give one of their children to childless relatives or to *compadres/comadres* (godparents). Pedro was given to his godmother and her husband at age five. Shortly thereafter, Pedro and his new parents moved to the Philippines. Joe has not seen his twin brother since. With a touch of emotion, he showed me a photograph of Pedro taken a few years after his move. The family resemblance was obvious.

Both of his parents emigrated from the Visayan island of Leyte and settled in Vallejo. His father, an imposing, light-skinned Filipino-Spanish *mestizo* (mixed), was employed at the Mare Island Naval shipyard for 35 years. He had other business pursuits as well—working as a bartender and bouncer in the evenings.

According to Joe, however, his father's most interesting business was running "a little whorehouse in our basement for lonely Filipino sailors." Vallejo was a bustling port during World War II. Busy Georgia Street, where his father often worked nights, was a popular hangout for the many Filipino sailors stationed on navy ships at the nearby Mare Island piers. After being asked by sailors on numerous occasions, "Where can I find a place to bring girls?" Joe's father decided he might as well create a business of his own. The empty basement was converted into several sleeping rooms to accommodate the Filipino sailors. When they brought girls to their rooms, his father turned the other way as he pocketed a healthy "tip" from the grateful sailors.

Unlike his father, Joe's mother Soledad was quieter and left the talking to her more gregarious husband. Her retiring manner may also have been due to the fact that she didn't speak English well—due perhaps to her secluded childhood in the rugged hills of her native Leyte.

Joe's parents divorced after twenty years of marriage in 1934, when Joe was eight—the beginning of eight years of a back and forth existence for Joe. At first, he remained in Vallejo with his father while Burt went to live with their mother. But his mother who had remarried and was residing in Salinas, missed him greatly. As a result, Joe often lived in Salinas for what usually were short periods of time. His mother and labor contractor stepfather insisted that he learn the value of work. Joe found himself working alongside *manongs* in the lettuce, tomato, and celery fields surrounding Salinas—the "Salad Bowl of America," Each time he worked in the fields, Joe grew adamant, "I wasn't born to work in the fields," he insisted. Not surprisingly, he seldom stayed in Salinas for very long.

His frequent visits to Salinas were nevertheless significant. It was there that he joined the Filipino American Youth Club of Sacred Heart and met many other Bridge Generation Filipinos. Among them were Sam and Jimmy Garcia who recruited the athletically gifted Joe to play on the club's basketball and softball teams. Salinas was a regular participant on the Filipino basketball tournament circuit, which gave Joe another opportunity to broaden his circle of friends. He also was skilled as a volleyball slammer at Filipino farm worker camp competitions, which always drew cries of *boomba* whenever he would jump high for a scoring spike.

At the outset of World War II Joe dropped out of high school and immediately tried to join the armed services but at sixteen was too young. Ever resourceful, Joe lied about his age and joined the Merchant Marine, which was known to be less strict in its scrutiny. Aboard ship, he learned to gamble from the *manongs*—Chinese pai que, Filipino rummy, and other games. Among his shipmates were a number of young Filipino Americans from Stockton who persuaded him to go to their hometown after their contract with the merchant marine was over.

The Stockton Filipino Catholic Youth Society Padres, hearing that Joe was now living in their community, immediately recruited him to play on its basketball team. The Padres was the third youth club team for which he performed. It would not be the last. Before Joe hung up his basketball shoes, he would go on to also play for Wilmington, the Stockton Filipino Youth Association, and the Vallejo Val-Phi. While we didn't know if such records were ever kept by the youth club basketball circuit, Joe and I agreed that playing for that many teams must be a record.

For years, Stockton young people, such as Ray Paular and Terry Rosal, had been going to Alaska during the summer to work in the salmon canneries. Working conditions were hard but the money was good and helped to support their families and provide for college. They convinced Joe to go with them. So for three summers during the mid 1940s, Joe became an *Alaskero*. Joe was appalled at the segregated conditions that Filipinos had to endure at the canneries. As a fair-skin *mestizo*, he was not always taken for a minority person by a society prone to think stereotypically. But Joe had seen many "No Filipinos Allowed" signs in Stockton. He had also experienced miscegenation when a *mestizo* friend and his *pinay* girlfriend were denied a marriage license because the authorities refused to believe that his light-skinned *mestizo* friend was half Filipino. However, the segregation of Filipinos in jobs and housing by the fish canneries in Alaska was the most flagrant example of discrimination he had ever personally experienced.

It was now more than ten years since Joe left home. These were carefree years. The money he made in Alaska would usually carry him for most of the year. And while he never appeared to have difficulty in finding work, he seldom worked at the same job for long or stayed in the same line of work. In addition to working in Alaska and old haunts in Vallejo and Salinas, he periodically went to Southern California.

For much of this time Stockton had become Joe's main base of operations. There were "many guys to hang around with and girls to date." Stockton was also where Joe continued his interest in *pai que*, a Chinese game played with domino-like tiles, and Filipino rummy. He also would *pusta* (bet) on the fighting roosters at the Sunday *sabongs* (cockfights).

Dancing had long been one of his passions. So when there was not a tournament dance to attend, he frequented the taxi dance hall in Manila Town. In one of those twists of fate, it was where Joe first met his future mother-in-law, a taxi dancer who was married to a Filipino—except he didn't know it at the time. He had yet to meet her daughter—his future wife.

The marriage to the taxi dancer's daughter was the first in what would eventually be six unions. It was also the only time Joe would marry a *pinay*; the others all being Caucasian. With the exception of the last marriage, all were of short duration, presumably because of Joe's difficulty in avoiding his carefree ways.

Joe suddenly grew sentimental as he began talking about June, his sixth wife. Originally from England, June was tall, Irish, and redheaded. Given Joe's passion for dancing, it was not surprising to learn that they met at a dance. Dancing was a passion that they both shared and participated in regularly. The compatibility in their dancing was reflected in their successful marriage of twenty four years during which time Joe was able to refrain from the carefree ways of his past. Sadly, June passed away several years ago. She was a union official in nearby Oakland and had invested well. "She paid off the condo, the cars, all the bills—I'm comfortable." says Joe gratefully.

Joe had a long and successful career as a supervisor with the Bay Area Rapid Transit System (BART). In 1996, Joe retired from BART after 27 years of employment. Mischievously, Joe winked as he confessed, "When they were applying for a job, I helped Filipinos more than *puti* (whites)."

His days on the basketball and volley ball courts may be over but he continues to be an avid golfer—as he has for the past forty years. At reunions, he is usually one of the first to enter the golf competitions. In addition to the many courses in California, he makes trips to golf courses to Nevada, often with Burt. And, he happens to live adjacent to the Metropolitan Golf Links in San Leandro.

In reflecting back on his life, Joe talked about the values he learned from his parents—be proud of being Filipino, be respectful, learn how to cook, keep yourself clean, be a good housekeeper, work hard, eat lots of vegetables, and dress neatly. From all indications, Joe has learned well.

JULIA OLIMPIO ARRO

"I Can't Stand Still"

Long before I had even thought of writing a book on the Bridge Generation, Julia had asked if I would be willing to help her develop her life story. So when I decided to include a segment on "Ordinary Yet Extraordinary" Filipino Americans as part of this book, Julia's story was an obvious fit—a win-win situation. Julia readily consented to be interviewed. In 2002 she and Phil, her husband of fifty five years, moved to the upper middle-class Sacramento suburban community of Cameron Park after many years of living in the small coastal town of Davenport, located equidistant between San Francisco and Santa Cruz.

Julia is now legally blind. As her sight began to fail, she and Phil realized they needed to be closer to good quality care. The move to Cameron Park fit the bill perfectly. Not only was quality medical care readily available, they also would again reside in the greater Sacramento area where they still had many relatives and friends. After selling their extensive holdings in Davenport, the couple purchased three new two-story houses in Cameron Park as investment property, moving into one for their new residence.

I've always regarded Julia as a high energy person, very involved in her community. It was not until our interview, however, that I realized the extent of her energy and involvement.

Julia was born on March 15, 1935 in the Central Coast town of Watsonville, California, the eldest daughter of Emilio Olimpio from the Philippine island of Leyte and his wife, Encarnacion, born and raised in Spain. Her father followed a circuitous route in immigrating to America. He first landed in New Orleans but shortly thereafter went to Mexico with a close friend. (In one of those ironical twists of fate, the friend married a Mexican woman who later would become the mother of Julia's sister-in-law Dora—the wife of husband Phil's brother, Bobby.) From Mexico, Julia's father traveled to Los Angeles, working as a cook and card dealer—eventually winding up in Watsonville where he met and wed Encarnacion.

On the other hand, Julia's mother took a more direct route to America. Immigrating with her parents, she went from Spain to Watsonville during the late 1920s. Julia's maternal grandparents, relatively well-off in Spain, had sold their property before coming to America. They invested the proceeds by buying up much of the property alongside Watsonville's main thoroughfare of Bridge Street. The purchase proved to be a wise investment, enabling Julia's grandparents to bring many of their Spanish relatives to Watsonville.

Julia's grandparents also invested in other properties. Soon after the onset of World War II, they took over the property of a Japanese farmer—forcibly sent to relocation camp by order of the government—in nearby Santa Rita and had Julia's parents farm it. Julia, seven years old at the time, remembers picking strawberries after coming home from school. While living in Santa Rita, she met the woman who was the model for the Aunt Jemima of cereal fame. "Aunt Jemima" lived down the road in a big house owned by a white man who drove "the biggest limousine" Julia had ever seen. She still has a photograph taken with her to commemorate the occasion. Julia also remembers going to a church with "Aunt Jemima."

> Just across the street was a Holy Roller church that "Aunt Jemima" attended. I went there once. It's really true what they say about those churches. They holler and yell. They even had me doing it too.

Several years later Julia's family left Santa Rita to manage family property in Davenport. The property consisted of three houses and was located just across Highway 1 with a view of the Pacific Ocean. When the nearby store became available in 1949, it too was purchased by Julia's grandparents and turned over to Julia's parents to operate. Working at the store when she was fourteen was her first experience in handling money—an experience that would prove to be most helpful in her later employment with banks.

Julia first met her future husband in 1946. Phil, recently discharged from the U.S. Army after seeing combat in the Philippines, was living with his sister in Davenport. Their friendly relationship would develop into a serious romance and in 1953, Julia and Phil were married in Reno. During the initial years of their marriage, Phil's employment with the government as an inspector led to a series of back and forth moves among various bases and ports in Sacramento, Stockton, and Oakland. Fortunately, moving expenses were picked up by the government. In the meantime, they had already started their family that would eventually grow to three boys and a girl. As busy as the moves and care for the children may have kept Julia, she also managed to obtain an Associate of Arts degree at Delta College and complete her studies in education at the University of Pacific—both in Stockton—to launch her teaching career.

Throughout her marriage, Julia was not a stranger to working in the fields. Earlier she picked strawberries and bunched carrots. Even a teaching career would not end working in the fields; now Julia also found time to thin lettuce and harvest onions. She also worked in the tomato canneries. "I can't stand still," says Julia. "My kids called me Super Mom."

Julia taught for seventeen years at St. George's School, teaching grades one through eight at least once in that span of time. During her last few years at the school she was assigned to the new Head Start Program. St. George is located in South Stockton, home to many Filipinos families and businesses. So perhaps it was not surprising that Julia and Phil would become heavily involved with the Filipino community and generous with their time and money. Beginning as a model at various fashion shows to raise funds for the school and for the Head Start Program, Julia soon became involved in fund raising events for the Filipino Community Center. She and Phil also contributed to the Center and were among the proud Filipinos in attendance at the Center's dedication ceremony in 1973. The building still stands in the midst of El Dorado Street's "Little Manila", a proud testament to Filipinos who helped settle Stockton.

Their involvement with the Filipino community continued following Phil's job relocation to the Port of Oakland. The family settled in nearby El Cerrito where Julia's cousin served as the mayor. In recognition of their work on behalf of the Stockton Filipino Community Center, the mayor recruited Julia and Phil as volunteers in building a similar community center for El Cerrito.

El Cerrito was also the location of Julia's banking career. She worked for three different banks for the next nine years, gaining valuable experience in virtually all banking functions. Her most interesting assignment was in ferreting out counterfeit money. Once, her skills resulted in a three million dollar confiscation of fake money, which sent the gang of counterfeiters to prison. She enjoyed her years in banking. However, Julia's banking career came to an abrupt end after receiving a bomb threat. The incident resulted in her suffering a ministroke as well as constant anxiety. She vividly recalls:

> All of a sudden, the police arrived. They found that it was a live bomb and took steps to defuse it. Phil also was there with people from the Port of Oakland. I have never been so scared in my life.

The traumatic bomb threat incident led to a return to Davenport in 1977. Julia and Phil purchased the old family property consisting of a store, eight houses, and an apartment building. In the following years, they built up a thriving business on the property that would house a post office, delicatessen, restaurant, beauty salon, offices, and a gas station. The subsequent addition of whale watching proved to be a profitable venture. Bus loads of tourists regularly stopped for a glimpse of whale herds as they passed through on their annual migration. Once, actress Loni Anderson was almost left behind—so fixated was she with watching the whales.

Julia and Phil were generous in sharing their business success with Davenport, regularly sponsoring and contributing to community functions, even after their move to Cameron Park. Their generosity was not limited to Davenport. A two-bedroom house trailer was donated to Cal Poly and a thirty-foot boat to the United Cerebral Palsy charitable organization.

Julia's father is mestizo Spanish, which makes Julia three-quarters Spanish. Regardless, she proudly identifies herself as "half and half Spanish and Filipino" in recognition of the significant role that Filipino culture has had on her life. Phil is a quarter Spanish, resulting in their children being three-quarters Spanish. Not surprisingly, her children also proudly identify themselves as Julia does—"half and half Spanish and Filipino."

As a light skinned mestiza, Julia rarely encountered discrimination. However, she has experienced it indirectly. While employed with an El Cerrito bank, Phil dropped in to cash a check. Upon his departure, Julia was summoned to the manager's office who asked, "Who was that?" Upon learning that Phil was her husband and that she was part Filipino, the manager said, "I thought you were Italian." Julia waited to report the incident to the district manager and resigned in protest.

Julia may have slowed a step or two because of blindness. However, she continues to be very much involved in her community. At Cameron Park, she continues her affiliation with the Elk's Club and keeps in touch with her old community of Davenport. As she says, "I can't stand still."

HILDO "SONNY" POMICPIC, JR.[3]

"Athlete and Sabongero"

With the exception of the four years he served with the Air Force, Sonny has lived in the Livingston, California area for all of his life. Born in the county seat of Merced, his first few years of life were spent in the nearby hamlet of Stevenson. He grew up in the Livingston countryside and for more than thirty years has resided on a quiet street in this small rural Central California town. A widower and with his children out of the house and on their own, Sonny now lives alone in a comfortable, well kept home where he and his wife Terry raised their family of four. Shy almost to a fault, he wasn't sure why his life story would be of interest to anyone but readily launched into our interview.

As a fellow Livingston "homie," I've known Sonny for as long as I can remember. Our families were close. Because my mother is his *ninang* (godmother), Sonny is my *igsu* (godbrother). His father, Hildo Sr., from the tiny Visayan island of Siquijor, was recruited as a *sakada* contract worker in Hawaii. It was there that he first met my father. Like many other Filipinos, he later immigrated to California during the 1920s. Between farm worker jobs in the Central Valley, Manong Hildo worked in a lumber mill in the foothills community of Sonora where he again ran into my father. They both subsequently settled in the Livingston area where their friendship would endure for the next fifty years.

Sonny's mother, Juanita Hernandez, was born and raised in El Paso, Texas, just across the border from the State of Chihuahua, Mexico, her ancestral home. During a visit to Arizona, she met Hildo Sr. who at the time was field packing lettuce. Apparently his father made an immediate impression and persuaded her to return with him to California. His mother was not quite prepared for the thick fog that greeted her upon her arrival. She wanted to go back to the sunny climes of Texas. However, with the advent of warmer weather and, most importantly, the birth of Sonny in 1936, she soon forgot about her homesickness and successfully adjusted to her new life. Not only did she adjust to California but *Manang* Juanita also adjusted to Filipino culture, learning to cook traditional Filipino food and quickly grasping the nuances of the Cebuano dialect spoken by her husband and friends. As a speaker of Spanish, English, and Cebuano, she was the first tri-lingual person I ever knew.

As a young boy going to Filipino family celebrations, Sonny remembers:

> There was always plenty of food and playmates at these large gatherings. This is where my friends and I would play, or, if we were in need of some cash, sing. My friend, Filemon (Andam) and I would sing together. We were a hit at many of the celebrations and were so good that the old Filipinos would throw pennies at us. We didn't know any Filipino songs, so we would sing patriotic songs we learned in school . . . in the 1940s, fifteen cents was worth a lot.

Fishing was another of Sonny's fond growing up memories.

> During the salmon (spawning) season, my father and I would go to the river and spear salmon. This was in the 1940s when salmon was abundant (but illegal to catch). We would go to the river, and he would spear as many salmon as he could. We would then take them back to the farm, clean and cut them into long strips, and dry them in a smokehouse, which was the equivalent of a small shack . . . [the salmon] had a salty, chewy taste to it and reminded me of beef jerky except with a fishy taste. I enjoyed the trips to the river with my father more than the salmon itself.

His father often took Sonny and his brother Fred with him on fishing trips to the Delta, a two hour drive. There, they would rent a boat for the day. Lunch was when they caught striped bass, which were cut up into small chunks of *kinilaw* (raw fish marinated with vinegar, soy sauce, and red peppers), eaten with the steamed rice they brought from home. "The best fish I have ever tasted," says Sonny. They were successful fishermen and never went without their tasty *kinilaw* lunch.

Sonny was arguably the best Bridge Generation athlete in the history of Livingston High School. He became a starter on both the varsity basketball and baseball teams in just his sophomore year and went on to earn all-conference and all-star honors during his three years of high school competition. As a 5'11" guard on the basketball team, Sonny was a masterful ball handler who often was called upon to dribble away the final minutes of the game—ala Meadowlark Lemon of Harlem Globetrotters fame. On the school baseball team, he was a hard-hitting first baseman, batting clean-up for the championship team.

His athletic success in high school was undoubtedly aided by playing for the Livingston Filipino American Youth Association Dragons when he was only eleven years of age. At the time Sonny was five to eight years younger than his teammates but at nearly his full height of just under six feet, he was a raw talent.

Self deprecating as usual, he remembers, "Even though I was one of the tallest, my skills were not as good as the other players, but they still let me play once in a while." Sonny quickly absorbed the rough and tumble brand of Filipino American youth club tournament play and greatly benefited from competing with and against older, more experienced players. Joining the Dragons came at a fortuitous time. The club immediately dominated in softball tournament play as Sonny, along with his 6'1" brother Fred, and Hank Dacuyan comprised a formidable pitching staff. In basketball, Sonny's ball handling helped the Dragons become among the more competitive teams in the youth club circuit. As in high school, Sonny's performances earned him a number of tournament all-star honors in both sports.

Sonny's athletic talents were nurtured at a young age. During the 1940s-50s, softball was the most popular leisure-time activity in Livingston where men's league games were scheduled on most nights and weekends. His father regularly brought Sonny and Fred to the softball games. "I picked up the game quickly and became quite a pitcher," says Sonny, "even pitching for a men's team while still in grammar school."

Like other Bridge Generation youth in the Livingston area, Sonny spent summer vacations picking grapes, apricots, and peaches. He prided himself on his work ethic and remembered making up to $20 a day picking peaches and drawing praise from more experienced *manongs*. But like other youth, he didn't see any of the money. Except for what he needed for clothes for the coming school year, the money he earned all went to his parents to help with family expenses, which by this time numbered eight children.

Sonny developed a strong interest in the Filipino pastime of *sabong* (cockfighting) when he was a teenager. His father and uncles always had fighting roosters of their own at home. Sonny was handy and available and helped them care and train the roosters for weekend cockfights. When he reached his teens, he already had his own stable of four roosters that he raised from the time they were chicks. He trained them regularly through a regimen of sparring and mock fights (without knives) until they reached fighting trim—similar to the way boxers were trained for upcoming bouts. At the *sabong* he was the *sabongero* (handler) in the ring who held his rooster while it and the opposing cock alternately pecked at each other to a fighting fury. At a signal from the referee of *larga* (go), he placed his rooster down on the ground with the hope that it would be the only survivor in a fight that surely would be fatal for one of the contestants.

While Sonny considered himself to be a proficient *sabongero* (trainer of fighting roosters), he never quite mastered the art of attaching the sharp knives to the rooster's leg. His father took care of that sensitive step. Sonny's interest in *sabong* was mainly for sport. He says, "I never had enough money to place serious bets on my roosters." It's been many years since Sonny has been a *sabongero* but he can still remember the excitement of competition that the sport gave him.

Along with his Bridge Generation buddy and classmate, Filemon Andam, Sonny enlisted in the Air Force for a four year hitch in 1956. The Air Force proved to be an eye opener from the outset. "For a small town Filipino boy, basic training provided many firsts in my life," he says. "It was my first time away from home, first time feeling so overworked, and my first experience with racism." He missed Filipino food so much that on his first day of leave in Texas, he ordered a bowl of rice with soy sauce. He also recalls being refused admission to a movie in Fort Worth and not being served in a restaurant because they "did not serve colored people." Says Sonny, "I still remember the sick feeling I felt in the pit of my stomach."

The worst example of racism Sonny experienced in the service was at March Air Force Base in Riverside, California. At the time he was playing for a basketball team comprised entirely of black players and one Filipino—Sonny. During a game against an all-white team, the referees made many bad calls against his team, which nevertheless were ultimately overcome in a win. The next day, without warning or good reason, the team was officially dismantled by the commanding officer because "there were no whites on the team." Sonny felt terrible over the dismantling decision—not for himself but for his black teammates. For the first time, he would personally experience the same deep hurt of racism that his black teammates experienced.

While these were Sonny's first experiences with blatant, overt discrimination he was not surprised. He had already encountered discrimination in less obvious ways during his high school years. Despite his years of athletic stardom, he was never invited to parties thrown by his classmates. Nor did he feel free to date white girls. Such was the culture of the times.

Sonny's wedding to Terry, a pre-school teacher, in 1965 was the beginning of forty-two years of a happy marriage. According to Sonny, it was love at first sight. From the nearby city of Merced, Terry knew from the beginning that here was the man she wanted to marry. Despite deep feelings for her, Sonny was not so sure that he was ready for marriage. But after going together for eighteen months, he became convinced and has never looked back. The marriage produced four wonderful children and five grandchildren—to whom Sonny is totally devoted.

Perhaps as important, marriage settled him down. After twenty-eight years of single life, Sonny began to take his work at the local Foster Farms poultry plant much more seriously. After achieving success at several different work assignments, he became the company's top-rated truck driver with a perfect accident-free safety record that earned him several all-expense paid vacations. He worked for forty-two years at Foster Farms before his retirement in 2007.

Marriage also has contributed to expanding Sonny's cultural identification. Although his mother was of Mexican heritage, he was raised as Filipino and identified himself as such for the first half of his life. But after marrying Terry, a Mexican American, in 1965 Sonny became more exposed to his other culture. He now is more understanding and appreciative of his mestizo self. At the same time Sonny admits, "I will never give up *kinilaw* and eating steamed rice with my meals."

Wilma Bucariza Aguinid[4]

"Rocky Mountain High"

As the wife of Alex Aguinid, the eldest son of old family friends, I've known Wilma for years. However, it was only recently that I learned of the fascinating story of her growing up years. The only daughter of the only Filipino family in town, she is the only Filipina American that was born and raised in Whitefish, Montana—a small railroad town located in the Rocky Mountains at an elevation of 3000 feet near Glacier National Park. When I was searching for contributions for the book, Wilma's story appeared to be a natural. But when I approached her for an interview, she said, "My life story is boring." I thought differently, and after some persistence on my part, she decided to share her story by writing a heartfelt manuscript. Hopefully, the following paragraphs will do justice to her story.

Wilma was born on May 25, 1932 in Whitefish, Montana, as were two younger brothers, Joseph and William—the children of Venancio Labrado Bucariza and Demetria Cabanero, both of Talisay, Cebu. In those days Whitefish's population was only 2000. Demographically, the town consisted largely of Pennsylvania Dutch (German), Italian, and Canadian Native Americans, plus three Japanese truck farming families and one Filipino family—the Bucariza's. The only other Filipinos the family would see was when migrant workers, periodically traveling by rail from California to toil in Montana's sugar beet fields, having heard by word of mouth that a Filipino family lived in Whitefish, stopped by to share a home cooked Filipino meal.

Wilma likened Whitefish to the old TV show *Mayberry,* which starred Andy Griffith. Says Wilma,

> We rented a house from the Japanese, situated on the river just below the Great Northern Railroad roundhouse. It was a snug little house with a wood burning stove and a cook stove. We bathed in a large galvanized wash tub. We had to go potty either in an arinola (bedpan) indoors or to the outhouse.

In a few years the family "moved a little closer to town where the neighbors were white folks." (It was hoped the neighbors' close proximity would help Wilma's mother improve her English.) In 1937 Wilma's parents purchased a one-bedroom house. "Mama knew how to stretch a dollar so eventually we were able to add two bedrooms so the boys could share one room and my uncle the other. I slept on a cot bed at the foot of my parents' room," recalls Wilma.

For Wilma's parents, the path from Talisay, Cebu to Whitefish, Montana was a long and circuitous one. Her father first immigrated to America when he was nineteen, arriving in Seattle in November 1919. He was able to obtain a job with the Great Northern Railroad working on a road gang that maintained the rails between Seattle, Washington and Minneapolis, Minnesota. In 1926 *Manong* Vanancio saved enough money to return to Talisay to court and subsequently wed Wilma's mother, Demetria Cabanero.

However, life in the Philippines was not easy. "Daddy's money ran out about 1928; Mama sold a hectare of land she inherited from her grandmother so Daddy could return to America. At Whitefish he worked at his old job with the railroad from 1928 to 1931 and again returned to the Philippines to bring back my Mama," says Wilma.

Her parents sailed to America aboard the steamship President Jefferson in March 1932. The trip must have been difficult for her mother since she was already into her last trimester of pregnancy with Wilma. According to Wilma, however, her mother never spoke of any difficulties regarding her pregnancy while at sea. Fortunately, the month long cruise went without incident. In describing her mother's arrival in Whitefish, Wilma recounts, "Her dream was to come to America, the land of gold, so you can imagine her amazement at seeing snow for the first time. She exclaimed, 'It's true, America is so rich they throw sugar all over the land.'"

Wilma's early years were during the Great Depression. "We didn't consider ourselves poor. We were working class—as were our neighbors," explains Wilma.

> One never had to ask for help, they were always there. In the fall, it was a ritual to have several cords of wood delivered in the alley. Our neighbors would come help us stack our wood in the woodshed. Then the following week, we would turn out to help the neighbors with their supply. Folks were so nice and trusting we never had to lock our doors. Try doing that nowadays!

Wilma's parents did not go beyond the fourth grade in the Philippines but were adamant that their children take full advantage of American education. Wilma remembers,

> They didn't let us get summer jobs (like a paper route or babysitting) because they wanted us to concentrate on studies. I'm ashamed to say that my brothers and I only finished high school and didn't have the desire to further our education, even though our teachers were always encouraging us. But for my folks, they were always proud of us. I remember that Daddy would sneak off work for a few hours in the spring to attend our song and dance programs. I remember peering out into the darkened auditorium to see if Daddy was silhouetted standing in the entrance doorway to watch me.

Her parents also wanted their children to be "true Americans". Wilma writes,

> To that end, they would speak to us in Visayan and we had to answer in English, so it was a two way learning experience. I remember sometime around 1949, our parents started studying to get citizenship papers. . . . I hated having to drill them every day after school. . . . It took mom only one try to pass, but the judge would not award her the paper until Daddy passed the exam. It took him three tries—so finally the judge must have felt sorry for Daddy and passed him. You see, Daddy memorized the study book—so if the questions were worded or phrased differently, he did not know how to answer. His English was limited to mostly, "Yeah, Yeah" and he would always smile.

Her mother had certain rules regarding Wilma's relationships with her school friends but Wilma would usually find ways to get around them.

> Mama was so strict about us kids coming home if our friends' parents were starting to cook; and we couldn't go on sleepovers. But at least on Sunday mornings we could see my best friend's uncle who lived across the alley from us. He would start his wood stove and make pancakes, sausages, scrambled eggs, chocolate milk and then he would stand at the kitchen door and call us and his nieces to eat breakfast with him.

Another example:

> On the way to school, my girlfriend and I would stop at her dad's taxidermist shop to ask for money (ostensibly for school supplies) but really to spend at the candy store. Sometimes he would give it to her. If not, we'd go to the inner room where the mounting was done and ask her uncle. If he was not forthcoming, we'd go into the back room where the hides were soaking in formaldehyde (phew) and beg another uncle who would usually hand us some coins. After school, we'd go through the same ritual because we wanted to go to the soda fountain before heading home. We did this about three times a week all through elementary school. If my mom ever found out I'd sure get a licking.

Wilma enjoyed school.

> I was always voted in as secretary, but I was too shy to campaign for office of president or vice president. I was even surprised when someone pledged me to be a Rainbow girl because I thought one had to have a mother in the Eastern Star (a Masonic women's organization).

Following Wilma's graduation from high school in 1950, the family moved to Stockton because of her mother's chronic health issues of having to live in the cold climate of Whitefish. The sunshine in California resulted in almost immediate improvement in her mother's health. However, Wilma did not fare as well and felt out of place in Stockton. She had close friends in Whitefish. She didn't know anyone her age in Stockton, except for her cousins. And as eager as she was to meet other Filipino youth, it was difficult to do so in a city in which she had not attended school. Through her younger brothers, she heard the names of Filipino young people from long established Stockton families. Years later, she was able to put faces to the names after her marriage to Alex and after joining the Filipino American National Historical Society. Wilma has often thought it was ironical that while she had many close friends in Whitefish which had no other Filipinos, in Stockton, which had the highest per capita population of Filipinos in the country, she was unable to establish similar relationships with her Filipino American contemporaries.

Going to business school and subsequent employment went a long way to effectively deal with Wilma's relative absence of close friends. She worked as a clerk typist for the federal government at Sharpe Army Depot in Stockton and later transferred to McClellan Air Force in Sacramento as a statistical clerk.

Moreover, her marriage to Alex in 1954 was of considerable help in making many new Filipino American friends. Alex, who served in the First Filipino Regiment of the U.S. Army during World War II and who came from a large family, had well established roots in heavily Filipino populated communities such as Salinas, San Francisco, Stockton, Livingston, and Sacramento. It did not take long for the outgoing and friendly Wilma to form lasting friendships.

During the relatively idyllic life in the small town of Whitefish, Wilma was spared the hurt of discrimination. In another bit of irony, however, the only incident of discrimination she experienced was perpetrated by her own people. Soon after their move to Stockton, the family, accompanied by cousins, was on their way to eat at a Chinese restaurant when she and her mother were suddenly spat upon by two *manongs*. The cousins scolded the two men, telling them that Wilma and her mother were *pinays*. After apologizing, the *manongs* explained they and their families had greatly suffered during the World War II occupation of the Philippines and had mistaken Wilma and her mother as Japanese. Regardless, the men's hatred toward Japanese left Wilma with mixed feelings—some of her best friends in Whitefish were Japanese.

Wilma's "five minutes of fame" came about when the national publication *Woman's World* magazine featured her in its December 1999 issue. It seems that she had wanted to reach an old Whitefish friend that she hadn't seen since 1950. She didn't have her friend's street address so she simply wrote her friends name and Whitefish, MT on the envelope with a note: "Haven't seen her in 49 years, but please try to send this—it's a small town and her family is prominent." The postman immediately found Wilma's friend. After the story appeared in the local paper, the magazine published her story.

During her children's school years, Wilma was active with the school's PTA, serving in several positions and eventually rising to the presidency. She also volunteered in classrooms and the library. However, now that her own children are grown and she no longer has young grandchildren to care for, she has busied herself by making quilts for the LINUS project whose motto is: "Providing security through handmade blankets for children in need." She also is a regular donor of blood, to which she quips, "Can you imagine Caucasians with Filipino blood in their system?"

Wilma's other current passion is the Filipino American National Historical Society. She was an original member of FANHS' Santa Clara Valley chapter upon its establishment in the early 1990s and subsequently contributed several articles to the chapter's journals.

But while Wilma has called California home for the past 58 years, she will be forever grateful for the unique experience of growing up brown in white Whitefish, Montana.

Virginia Garcia Randall[5]

"I Held My Own With the Guys"

"I never thought of being anything else than Filipino." Her strong ethnic identification is undoubtedly due to her growing up in the Central Coast community of Salinas, California. With the exception of Stockton, Salinas is believed to have had the highest number of Filipinos per capita during Virginia's formative years. Its main thoroughfare of Market Street teemed with Filipinos frequenting its shops and restaurants, particularly in the evenings and weekends.

Filipinos were the main source of labor for the Salinas Valley's extensive lettuce, cauliflower, and sugar beet industry. Unlike asparagus in the Stockton-Delta area which require large numbers of farm workers for five months, the crops in the Salinas Valley can keep workers busy the year around. Consequently, permanent rather than seasonal Filipino camps dotted Salinas and its surrounding landscape. Among those camps was the Garcia camp, located a few miles from town. The division of labor in operating the camp was typical of the times. As labor contractor, her father's primary responsibility was to assure that work was available for the workers. Her mother and children were responsible for feeding the men and for the upkeep of the camp.

The fourth child in a family of seven children, she credits her parents with instilling Filipino cultural values in their children, particularly her father. According to Virginia, while her father didn't talk extensively to his children, he communicated "what was important." His communications were not limited to Filipino culture. He also emphasized "ways to live as a person."

Growing up in a camp populated by *manongs* from the Visayan Islands of Panay, Siquijor, Cebu, Bohol, Negros, and Leyte proved to be an additional rich resource in learning about Filipino culture. To this day, Virginia can still remember the men's stories of their native land.

By the time she was a teenager, the family camp had relocated into the town of Salinas itself. The move brought Virginia into contact with many more Bridge Generation young people. One day, she and her friends were bemoaning the lack of activities for youth. Together with close friend, Sonny Majurocan, she decided to go to the local Catholic parish to request its sponsorship of a youth club. The Church consented. In 1948, the Salinas Filipino American Youth of Sacred Heart was born. Its establishment was timely. Other youth clubs were also being established across Northern and Central California, giving rise to Filipino American athletic tournaments. During her tenure, the Salinas fielded one of the more competitive basketball teams in the Filipino youth club circuit and hosted a number of weekend tournaments.

Virginia's only disappointment about the youth club was that these were the days before girl's basketball. Athletically inclined, she regularly practiced with members of the basketball team. She says proudly, "I held my own with the guys." Without a team to play on, Virginia turned increasingly to bowling—another sport in which she excelled. She carried a 168 average and for a time considered going professional.

Sports were not Virginia's only interest. Through her mother, Virginia and her four sisters were exposed to the finer things in life—culture. She vividly recalls taking music lessons and going to concerts. An early role model was a coloratura from Beverly Hills. She often sang for the girls and shared her experiences in the music world. A close personal friend of the family doctor, she visited Salinas often. Incidentally, it was the family doctor who gave Virginia music lessons. All he asked for in payment was for Virginia to help him with his halting English.

Music was not to be Virginia's vocation. Beginning with science classes in high school, she gravitated to becoming a chemist with her studies at Hartnell College in Salinas and at Dominican College in San Rafael, just north of San Francisco. She has been happy with her choice of a profession. Being a chemist has enabled her to live the good life. Perhaps as important it led to her meeting her future husband, John Randall, also a chemist. John went to work for the Spreckles Company in Salinas—the company that Virginia had been working for following her graduation from Dominican College. They wed in 1969 after a brief courtship.

Virginia and John still work together but for a different company in the East Bay. Through the years they have traveled extensively. Virginia says, "I must have really been insulated in all the years I lived in Salinas because the only incidents of discrimination I experienced happened during my travels." In Texas she encountered segregated water fountains. While vacationing in New Orleans she went to a hair salon and was immediately ushered to a back room. At first, Virginia didn't notice but as she looked around everyone in the back room was black. Indignantly, she walked out commenting, "I'm glad I don't live here."

In reflecting back on her life, Virginia feels "blessed by having understanding parents." Moreover, she is appreciative what her parents and immigrant Filipinos have gone through. "I'm thankful for their hospitality, their humor, and their generosity—being Filipino is truly a blessing."

RAYMOND ARCA PAULAR

"Auditor and Acting Warden"

My first brush with Ray was literally a "brush back." As teenagers we were competitors on opposing Filipino youth club softball teams—Ray was the star pitcher of the Filipino Youth Association of Stockton (FYA); I was playing second base and batting lead off for the Livingston Filipino American Youth Association Dragons. Relatively tall for a Filipino, Ray squinted down at me as he tried to figure out how to pitch to me—just over five feet in height. I was hunched over, trying to take full advantage of my short stature and hoping to coax a walk from Ray. His first pitch brushed me back from home plate. His second pitch hit me on the backside, sending me to first base. The teams would compete several more times during the next few years. Each time the result was the same. Ray would always hit me and I would gratefully trot over to first base. But to be fair, I was never able to get a base hit off the fast-pitching Ray. We didn't realize it at the time but our paths would intermittently but significantly cross for the next sixty years.

Ray is the eldest of four sons of Paul Paular of Carmona, Cavite Province and Felicidad Arca of Dumaguete City, Negros Oriental Province. Born on April 3, 1930 in Oakland, California he spent most of the first dozen years of his life in Los Angeles where the family lived in a mostly white but mixed neighborhood. There, Ray underwent a normal and uneventful life—developing an interest in music, playing ball, and horsing around with his brothers, Jerry and Paul Jr. (Corney was considerably younger at the time). The only untoward incidents he recalls were as a young paperboy when he was told, "You don't belong here," and during high school when white students at a scholarship club meeting similarly asked him, "Are you sure you belong here?"

The onset of World War II would bring profound changes for Ray:

> The world at that moment became a smaller place. I felt that I was beginning to leave my childhood behind. Shortly, the family moved to Stockton, where I spent my teenage and early twenties years and got more immersed in the Filipino American culture because we were now living in "Little Manila".

At age 12 Ray began toiling in the fertile fields surrounding Stockton. He sacked onions for twenty cents a sack, making $2.00 a day and picked grapes in nearby Lodi. He later picked grapes in Biola—near the Central California city of Fresno—where he had the unusual experience of sleeping on boxes next to a pig sty. At Biola he also was bitten by a nest of yellow jacket hornets that resulted in a painfully swollen face. With such misfortune, Ray decided that two weeks was enough and returned home to Stockton.

Ray's work force experience became more positive in 1946 when an uncle recruited him to work in the Alaska fish canneries. He was dismayed at the second class treatment of Filipinos—relegated to the most difficult jobs, endured crowded living quarters, and limited to "Filipino food"—compared to white cannery workers. Although the working conditions were not desirable, however, the lucrative pay was too good to pass up. For the next eight summers, Ray worked as an *Alaskero*, virtually providing all the money he would need to finish college.

Stockton was also where Ray was recruited to pitch for FYA. He was the youngest player on a softball team of older Bridge Generation Filipino Americans; many of them recently discharged ex-servicemen. While the team had plenty of candidates for the infield and outfield, it lacked a reliable pitcher. Ray filled the void nicely.

Softball was not Ray's only sport. He also became an amateur boxer. During the 1920-30s heyday of the *Manong* Generation, Stockton hosted many bouts of professional Filipino boxers, such as champions Ceferino Garcia and Speedy Dado. Inspired by their success, Stockton's Jimmy Florita became a popular drawing card for Stockton boxing fans during the late 1940s. Similarly inspired, a number of young Filipino American amateur boxers, including Ray, began to emerge in Golden Gloves competitions across California. After experiencing limited success, Ray's boxing career came to a sudden halt when he went away to college in 1949.

Ray enrolled at San Jose State (SJS) to pursue a degree in accounting. He initially considered majoring in music but after the professor listened to Ray perform on the piano, he was advised to "stick to accounting." Ray also encountered another incident of discrimination while at SJS. Responding to an ad for a part time job, he was told, "The job was filled." But when he telephoned back he learned the position was still open. Without a legal recourse to turn to, Ray wrote a letter to the school's daily paper only to be immediately chastised by the Dean of Men for "bringing shame to San Jose State College."

Ray went on to earn a BA in accounting at SJS in 1953. Later he was an MBA candidate at the University of California at Berkeley before his education was interrupted by being drafted into the U.S. Army.

The Korean War, which broke out in June of 1950, would prove to be another profoundly significant event for Ray—similar to that which transpired after the onset of World War II. He recalls:

The Korean War, for me, represented a transition into manhood for a lot of reasons—an earlier marriage that did not work out, a break-up of all the Filipino athletic teams up and down the state because of players going into the service, my eventual time in the Army which saw me going to Okinawa for a while, and breaking down with TB caused by pleural effusion and being confined to Fitzsimmons Army Hospital in Denver, Colorado for over a year. During lung surgery I hemorrhaged and was almost given my last rites but managed to survive. Needless to say, this was an" eye-opener" and gave me a whole new perspective about the meaning of life.

Ray's accounting degree led to a thirty-two year career with the State of California. Beginning as a junior accountant with the Youth Authority, he worked in various capacities for the Departments of Employment, Highways, and Mental Hygiene, before rising to the position of auditor with the Department of Corrections. From time to time, Ray briefly assumed temporary duties as Acting Warden in charge of prisons which held some of the most dangerous men in California. He is forever thankful that in his acting capacity he was never called upon to quell an uprising or deal with a serious inmate incident.

Since Ray's retirement from full time employment in 1991, he has worked as a seasonal tax preparer for H&R Block. However, most of his retirement time has been devoted to volunteering on behalf of the Filipino community. He is a charter member of the Sacramento Chapter of the Filipino American National Historical Society (FANHS), a former member of FANHS National Board of Trustees, a VIP (Very Important Pinoy) Silver Award winner, a committee member of several reunions of Filipino old-timers, and a recipient of the Filipino Community Leader of the Year award by the Sacramento Filipino Chamber of Commerce. Of particular personal pride to Ray was his work in helping to develop and market the 2005 TV film documentary *Untold Triumph: The Story of the First and Second Filipino Regiments.*

As to being a Filipino American, Ray has an interesting perspective and says:

> I consider myself Filipino American—without the hyphen because we are striving within ourselves not to be divided which the hyphen would suggest. I've always maintained that the "colonial mentality" in our people emanates first from the Spanish conquerors in the Philippines, then, the Americans, who used the technique of "divide and conquer" among our fore bearers for control purposes.

What is Ray's greatest achievement? "To be able to live long enough to celebrate fifty years of marriage with a great wife and to enjoy two beautiful daughters and three wonderful grandchildren.

ROBERT SAN JOSE, JR.

"Sportsman and Leader"

Filipino youth club basketball tournaments flourished in northern and central California during their heyday in the 1950s. Due to the great distance, it was rare for teams from southern California to participate. However, the Wilmington "Papayas", comprised of young Filipinos from the Los Angeles area, were able to make several trips north in the early 1950s. Their trips were successful as they beat most of the opposition, including one victory over the usually unbeatable San Francisco Mangos. It was on one of these trips—in a Stockton tournament—that I first met the friendly and outgoing Bob San Jose. We would not meet again until fifty years later when my wife Terri and I were invited to the City of Industry to consult with the organizers of the first Southern California reunion of Bridge Generation Filipino Americans.

The son of Robert San Jose, Sr. from the Visayan island of Cebu and Laura Lynch—half Irish, a quarter French, and a quarter American Indian—from Everett, Washington, Bob was born on May 16, 1934 in Long Beach CA. He grew up in nearby Wilmington but unlike the vast majority of his Bridge Generation contemporaries, his formative years were spent in white neighborhoods. As Bob describes it, "I grew up living in the Caucasian community—used to being one of the few non-whites in school." Likewise, his fifty-five year marriage to his high school sweetheart, Filipina American Janet Olarte, was spent in white neighborhoods.

> In the beginning, many of the clubs I belonged to and functions we attended, my wife and I were the only non-whites. I realized in my teens that the families and friends we had were all in mixed marriages. I feel that we, consciously or not, were bonded because we were not accepted by the whites nor Filipinos. This helped me grow up in a world of divided lives and ideas.

At the same time, much of Bob's early experiences were rooted in Filipino culture. When he was ten his parents became heavily involved in the Filipino community. "My parents were among the founders of building the Filipino Community of the Los Angeles Harbor Area in Wilmington," says Bob proudly. "It was the largest Filipino Community building owned by Filipinos in the country." Inspired by his parent's community involvement, Bob helped to establish the local Filipino teen club, becoming its first president. As an adult Bob later became the youngest—and only mestizo—to serve as president of the Filipino Community. It was his parents' turn to be proud.

In addition to playing basketball with the Wilmington Papayas, Bob was an all-city running back at Long Beach's Wilson High School before a serious knee injury ended his football career. The injury was so serious that it also kept him from entering the military service. An all around athlete, Bob also played softball and remembers his biggest thrill was, at age seventeen, being a teammate of some of southern California's most outstanding Filipino athletes. One of his teammates was Bobby Balcena of Long Beach—the first Filipino to play in baseball's major leagues as a centerfielder for the Cincinnati Reds.

It was in the sport of golf, however, that Bob was to become best known—first as a player, then serving in leadership positions, and finally working as a rules official with the Professional Golf Association and the U.S. Golf Association. "I thank my wife Janet for getting me into the golf world," says Bob. "She gave me a membership to the Skylinks Men's Club." Thus began a long association with golf. Beginning as president of the Skylinks, Bob would assume leadership positions with several clubs, including serving as president of the 10,000 member Public Links Golf Association of Southern California.

Golf allowed Bob to travel extensively and to play and work in some of the best courses in the world. His long and successful association with golf has also brought personal recognition as he was the recipient of many awards and honors. He is particularly proud of being named to the Long Beach Golf Hall of Fame in 2006; among the Hall's members is superstar Tiger Woods.

Bob's main day job was with the electric industry. Semi-retired, he still works periodically with fish canneries in far-off American Samoa. He and Janet are also regular attendees of Bridge Generation reunions, held in Northern and Southern California in alternate years, where friendships forged as youth can once again be renewed.

In reflecting back on his life, Bob says:

> I have been blessed with many honors, the love of families and friends. I have been able to see how it was before, how it has changed, and how it is today. I hope I helped make that change.

RIZALINE RAYMUNDO

"The Dutiful Daughter"

I first met Riz during the formative years of the Santa Clara Valley Chapter of the Filipino American National Historical Society (FANHS) in the early 1990s. At the time she was in the process of preparing a manuscript of her mother's diary. The diary, written in simple but vividly descriptive words by Riz's mother when she was just a young girl of 11-15, chronicled her family's migratory farm worker experiences in Hawaii and California during the 1920s. Excerpts were published in five issues of the chapter's *Filipino Journal* beginning in 1991. But Riz had more ambitious plans for her mother's diary, entitled *Tomorrow's Memories: Diary of Angeles Monrayo, 1924-1928*. She wanted it to be published in book form. The fact that she succeeded in having the University of Hawaii Press publish the book in 2003, is a testimony not only to Riz's perseverance, but also to her pride in her Filipino heritage.

Riz was born on July 14, 1929 in Modesto, California. She would be followed by the birth of a brother, Donald, two and a half years later. Her mother wanted to name Riz "RosaMaria" after her two closest friends in Hawaii; but somehow the county registrar typed her name "Rose Marie" on the birth certificate. It didn't really matter. The woman who was asked to be *ninang* (godmother) said "RosaMaria" sounded like "roast pork" to her and wouldn't consent to be godmother unless the name was changed. Finally, her father came up with the name of "Rizaline" for the baptismal certificate—the only given name Riz has ever used.

Riz's birth was only a few months before the 1929 Wall Street Crash which precipitated the Great Depression—America's worst economic downturn—a period that would last until the onset of World War II. At the time of the Crash, her family lived in the small San Joaquin Valley community of Oakdale working in the nearby peach orchards and grape fields. The ensuing Great Depression would begin nine years of a migratory farm worker existence for the Raymundo family. Riz remembers:

> my parents became migrant workers following the crops through the seasons. We traveled all over Central California—Modesto, Delano, Bakersfield, Visalia, Delta Area, and other places I can't remember. We lived in bunk houses, shacks, barns, tents, in an abandoned railroad junction and in a box car. We lived with friends or friends lived with us. We ate everything from chicken feet to fish heads, rice and mushroom, rice and mustard greens but thankfully fish was plentiful in the rivers.

For several winters, Riz's father worked in the Imperial Valley where the weather was more conducive for agriculture. The rest of the family stayed with friends. "Single men and families lived together in camps . . . supporting each other—whoever was fortunate to find a job, supported the others." says Riz. The *bayanihan* (community togetherness) spirit was alive and well. She recalls her mother saying the Filipino community at the time was close-knit and took care of one another—no one she knew was on welfare. To this day Riz still wonders how her parents and their friends ever made it through the Depression years.

The worst thing about the constant moves for Riz was going to so many schools and having to leave the few friends she may have made in the short time she lived in various localities. The family's move to Salinas in 1939 would put an end to their migratory life. "At least my brother and I were able to go to one elementary school and one high school instead of a different school every semester," says Riz. They joined the Salinas Filipino Youth Club and were able to make lasting friends. Riz was also active in high school—playing basketball, soccer, badminton, track, archery, and baseball and winning a school sweater and two letters in the process.

While their migratory life may have ended for Riz and Donald, their work in the fields did not. They worked in the lettuce fields alongside their parents during weekends and summer vacations. They also bunched carrots and hoed a variety of vegetables that were in great abundance in "America's Salad Bowl." Riz says, "It was awful to have to get up before the sun, to go out to the fields to work among cold, wet vegetables and when the sun came out, sweat dripped into your eyes while blessedly cooling off your body under your sweatshirt and jeans." However, the work in the fields had its rewards for Riz, "I hated field work but enjoyed going to the stores to buy a skirt, blouse, or a sweater."

The Raymundo family was to stay in Salinas for the next ten years, aided in large part after Riz's father obtained a job as an irrigator and tractor driver for Stolich and Company, one of the Salinas Valley's largest farms. He then began taking diesel mechanic classes at night. Coincidentally, his instructor was the chief mechanic at Stolich and Company and got him a job as a shop mechanic during the times when he was not driving tractor. The father's improved work situation enabled the family to move into a company house with an outside shower and outhouse. It was not ideal. However, it had three bedrooms. For the first time, Riz and Don would have their own bedrooms.

Riz's father, Alejandro Salvador Raymundo, was born in 1903 in Manila. At eighteen years of age he got a job as a waiter on a steamship bound for America—the SS Wenatchee—and disembarked in San Francisco. Like many Filipinos of the time, he was motivated by the glowing tales he heard of the opportunities available in America and fully intended to return to the Philippines a richer man. But like other Filipinos, he soon learned that because of discrimination and racism, the real America was far different. Disillusioned at not being able to achieve his goal but too proud to face friends and family in the Philippines, he would never return to his homeland.

Manong (a term of respect for an older Filipino man) *Alejandro* worked in a variety of jobs in which he had no previous experience—in a hospital dining room, in an Alaska salmon cannery, topping sugar beets, cutting asparagus, and selling tailored suits to other Filipinos—a veritable jack of all trades. "Everything he knew, he taught himself," says Riz. He learned how to play the violin, saxophone, and trumpet. He learned how to carve, paint, make furniture, and made his own fishing poles from scratch. Once, when there was no room at a farm labor camp for his family, he built a one-room house from lumber that mysteriously became available. According to Riz, the house leaned to one side but was nevertheless livable.

Riz's mother, Angeles Monraya, was born in 1912 on the tiny island of Romblon, just north of the large Visayan island of Panay. At three months of age, together with her mother and brother Julian, she sailed to Honolulu, Hawaii with her father, recruited as a *sakada* (Filipino laborer recruited by the Hawaiian Sugar Planters Association). Plantation life in Hawaii was a decided improvement from the uncertainties of the Philippines. Work was hard but steady. The plantation house was small but accommodating. When *Manang* (a term of respect for an older Filipina woman) *Angeles* was six years of age, however, her own mother (Riz's grandmother) ran off with another man to the island of Kawai, taking Riz's mother with her. By the time she was reunited with her father and brother Julian, *Manang Angeles* had already turned ten.

Life back with her father and brother meant that while he was away at work on the plantation, *Manang Angeles* and Julian were placed in the care of other families who didn't always provide the same level of care for them as they gave their own children. Luckily, *Manang Angeles* was self-sufficient, thanks to her own mother who taught her how to cook, wash, and care for herself during the four years she spent on Kawai. Years later, she would teach these same lessons of self-sufficiency to her daughter, Riz.

Riz's mother did not start school until she was ten years old. However, she proved to be a quick study, learning how to read and write well enough so that just a year later she began recording her everyday experiences in her diary. The first diary entry is particularly poignant:

Waipahu, Oahu T.H. January 10, 1924

Dear Diary:

Christmas and New Year is now over and the month of the beginning of the New Year of 1924, and I think this is the best time to start a diary—my teacher told us about a book that she wrote about herself. And this is why I got my idea to start one for myself, because I would like to read about me—what everyday things happen to me—when I am old woman, right now I am only 11 years, 5 months.

According to Riz, her mother always had a strong interest in reading and education—interests that were passed on to Riz. Her mother's education was aided by joining the 4-H Club in Honolulu. There, she found another venue to improve her reading and writing skills. She also learned how to prepare American food such as custard pie, meatloaf, cakes, and salads.

The Raymundo family soon would be caught up with a labor strike for better wages and living conditions led by Pablo Manlapit. Ultimately defeated by the plantation owners, many Filipinos were forced to go to California to seek work. The family left Hawaii for California in 1927. In Stockton, Riz's mother, just fifteen years old, found work as a table girl at a local pool hall on Market Street. It was there that her romance with Riz's father, then working as a salesman of tailored suits, blossomed. Within six months, they were married. A year and a half later, Riz was born.

Riz is now 79 years old, retired, and living in Lakeport, California. In reflecting upon what she learned from her parents, Riz says, "The struggles, hardships and hard work my parents had to endure taught me what hard work was and not complain but do the best I can." She went on to state, "To this day, for instance, I'll work in my yard during cold or hot weather not completely enjoying it but it was work I had to do to keep my yard clean and also clean my house—I don't much relish housework but it has to be done." In hearing Riz's words about work, I was reminded that these were almost the same words that her mother used as a teenaged bride in a 1928 diary entry.

Work was not always easy for Riz. She had her share of workplace discrimination in the years before there were civil rights protections or affirmative action programs. During the early '50s she worked at the San Francisco Naval Shipyard and was threatened with demotion for questioning why she had to do the work of her immediate supervisor. Only her subsequent letter to the Personnel Office giving her side of the issue prevented a demotion. Later, in following up her interview for a clerical position in Santa Clara County, she was told that she had turned down the job, when in fact she did not. In yet another example of discrimination, she was informed that the county did not have a vacancy for a position she had applied for when in fact there indeed was an opening. Riz also encountered several situations in which she believes she was unfairly overlooked for promotion.

Despite her experiences, Riz has an enlightened attitude regarding discrimination. "In my social life, if I came across discrimination, I just turned my back on it.... I only fought prejudice and discrimination if I thought it blatantly affected my life or job. Otherwise I'd ignore the people . . . it was their problem to be so narrow minded, not mine." As it turned out, Riz helped to fight prejudice and discrimination, for others, in the last two jobs Riz held with Santa Clara County—Secretary for the Commission on the Status of Women and Secretary for the Office of Human Relations. In a further twist of irony, had they existed at the time, these were precisely the kinds of programs that could have been of assistance to Riz earlier when she herself encountered discrimination in the workplace.

Riz also worked second jobs for a number of years which enabled her to buy a home in San Jose, which she described as "my proudest achievement . . . so that my parents would have permanence in their life, not moving from one job to another, following the seasonal crops."

Having her parents in her home had other benefits. It provided built-in child care for her daughter Patty, enabled her father to obtain permanent work with a box-making company, and later when Patty was a teenager provided an opportunity for *Manang Angeles* to work as a department store clerk.

Riz retired in 1995 after thirty-six years of employment with the County of Santa Clara to care for her mother who had lost her sight and had undergone several major surgeries. Retirement also afforded her the opportunity to complete work on her mother's diaries and reflect on her Filipino American heritage.

"Pride In Your Heritage Is Pride In Yourself" is how Riz entitled the material she submitted to me for her life story in August 2008. She considers herself as an "American Filipino—American with a heritage of Filipino, but I do not forget I am of Filipino descent and very proud of it." She owns a collection of Filipino stories and books and also completed a family genealogy. The establishment of the local chapter of the Filipino American National Historical Society in 1989, which she co-founded with Esther Navarro Romero, would greatly enhance the opportunities to learn more of her heritage. She provided articles for the chapter's *Filipino Journal,* serving as editor of several issues. As a member of the Santa Clara Valley chapter, she worked on the very successful 1994 FANHS National Conference in San Francisco.

So what does Riz believe is her greatest gift and tribute to her Filipino heritage? The 2003 publication of *Tomorrow's Memories: A Diary, 1924-28*—her mother's story of struggle in a migratory farm worker family in Hawaii and California.

GABINA HIPOLITO BOISER

"Babe"

It was the promise of a better life by the Hawaii Sugar Plantation Association recruiters in 1919 that enticed Leoncio (or Dodong as he was affectionately called), his wife Francesca, and many of their fellow Cebuanos to leave the Central Philippines island of Cebu to come to Hawaii. (Gabina was born in 1920 in Honolulu.) HSPA did not keep its promise. During the early 1920s, a series of strikes, led by Filipinos, ensued to protest their poor wages and squalid living conditions. In 1924 Hawaii, 1600 Filipino plantation workers staged an eight month strike. In the end the HSPA prevailed, forcing many Filipinos to flee to California in their continuing quest to seek a better life. Among those sailing to California were Gabina Hipolito, her parents, Leoncio and Francesca Hipolito, and her older brother Sussano.

The Hipolito family was met at the San Francisco docks by contractors and quickly whisked to Stockton—eighty miles away. There, they were to taken to a nearby camp where her father worked in the hot dusty fields cutting asparagus, where her mother served as camp cook, and where the young family shared an old bunkhouse located in the peat dust fields of the Delta with several dozen single Filipino farm workers.

Gabina, only four years of age in 1924, has only limited personal recollection of those events. However, she has plenty of other memories of the rest of her life—all of which was spent in California's San Joaquin Valley. I've known Gabina Hipolito Boiser, or "Babe" as she is better known among her relatives and friends, since 1936. Babe did not have any problem sharing her life story. We both laughed as she reminded me of my childhood crush on her when I was only six and she was sixteen; I followed her around every chance I could. Today, at 88 years of age and after eight children, she has not changed appreciably. Babe possesses the same girlish figure of her days as a *dalaga (*unmarried young woman*)*. She also still has the same shy demeanor. Looking nervously at the tape recorder on the table, she says softly, "I don't know why you want to interview me, I haven't done anything important."

Babe is the oldest daughter in a family that would eventually reach thirteen children. In order to better support his rapidly growing family, *Manong Dodong* got a job in 1928 as a labor contractor for Matt Jenkins, the millionaire rancher of grape fields and peach orchards in the Livingston area. The rancher provided housing for the family and for about twenty-five Filipino farm workers—all members of the Filipino Federation of America.

The Federation was an organization that drew its membership largely from *sakadas* (Filipinos recruited to work on Hawaiian plantations) who immigrated from Cebu and the neighboring islands of the Visayas in the Philippines. The organization's followers believed that *sacripisyo* (sacrifice) through fasting and abstinence would protect them from temptations, such as taxi dances and alcohol, which had befallen many *manongs* in America.

In the year before moving to Livingston, Babe's parents had joined the Federation, an affiliation that brought unexpected changes to the family's accustomed life style. She vividly recalls, "We couldn't eat meat—chicken and fish were okay. We couldn't have salt with our food either." After years of eating pork *adobo* and using soy sauce with their food, the children found it difficult to adjust to the Federation's rules. Her resourceful mother helped ease her children's loss somewhat by providing tomato sauce at the kitchen table—but it wasn't the same.

The Federation was not all rules and sacrifice for Babe and her siblings. Most of the men at the camp were also members of the Federation band. For weeks, the band would rehearse almost every evening for the big Fourth of July parade in Stockton—a welcome source of entertainment for the Hipolito children.

As a young girl, Babe often sang at home and at parties. When she was twelve, she sang at the national convention of the Federation in Los Angeles. The founder of the Federation, Hilario Moncado, was so taken with her singing that he offered to send her to music school—an offer that she and her parents turned down reluctantly. Babe attributed her musical talent to her father, a noted classical singer in Cebu.

Babe only went to the eighth grade. By then, there were nine children in the Hipolito family. As the oldest girl, Babe had to help with the kids as well as in the camp kitchen. Moreover, it was 1934—the midst of the Great Depression. Her sisters were also impacted by the Great Depression. While they were able to begin high school, they were unable to finish as they, like many other children during that time, had to work in the fields to supplement the family's income.

At the height of the Depression Babe's father contracted pneumonia and developed a heart condition—never to work again. With her father unable to work, the camp was soon disbanded. The family fell on even harder times in times that were already hard. The children all worked in the fields. With the onset of World War II, Sussano was drafted into the U.S. Army and Babe's younger brothers, Frank and Ben—then in their early teens—went away to Stockton to toil in the backbreaking asparagus fields.

In 1937 Babe married Albert Dublin, a prominent member of the Daguhoy Lodge of the Legionnarrios Del Trabajo, a Filipino Masonic organization. The wedding was a gala affair held in Stockton's Civic Auditorium. The festivities began with the couple walking under swords held by a long receiving line of lodge members dressed in their best Masonic finery. It was the most people that Babe had ever seen in one place.

Babe had met Albert through her godmother, Mama Polonia, a founding member of the Alonzo Teodora Lodge, the woman's auxiliary of the Daguhoy Lodge. Earlier, her godmother had recruited Babe into the lodge with the additional motive of having her participate in social box dances to raise money for the lodge. Babe was an immediate success, selling the most tickets in ultimately winning the title of Queen in her first attempt. When Albert expressed an interest in Babe, Mama Polonia served as chaperone—a must at a time when young *dalagas* were not allowed to be alone with suitors without being chaperoned. It was also her godmother who went to Babe's parents to inform them of his intention to marry her. Babe had no objections because, "I liked him too."

Typical of the times, Babe was not adequately prepared for marriage, sex, or motherhood. Her mother simply said, "Whatever God gives you, you take." No other advice was provided. Her parents' response was similar to the day she had her first menstrual period. Babe remembers crying out, "I'm bleeding, maybe somebody hit me." But her parents only laughed.

Babe's days of working in the fields were not over. Albert had a steady job caring for a ranch in Stockton. Between pregnancies, Babe worked side by side on the ranch with her husband. To help out she also worked in canneries, cut apricots and peaches at the dry yard, counted raisin trays during grape season, and got on her knees to harvest sweet potatoes.

Babe's first marriage ended in divorce when she learned of Albert's infidelity. By then she had three children. She moved back to her parents' home in Delhi, just north of Livingston. She would marry twice more—to Minisio Abastillas and Leonicio Boiser with five more children resulting from the two unions. Boiser was one of Babe's many suitors as a *dalaga*. At the time, her choice of a husband was between him and Albert. After Abastillas passed away, it was an easy decision for Babe to say "yes" to Boiser when he proposed in 1949. It was a happy marriage that only ended with his untimely death.

Perhaps because of her sheltered early life, Babe could not recall encountering racial discrimination directly. On the other hand, some of her comments appeared to reflect the stereotypical views of her parents' generation regarding blacks and Chinese.

At 88 years of age, Babe is pleased about how things have turned out for her. All but one of her eight children is in close proximity to her home, providing her with the opportunity to see them often. She has twelve grandchildren, four great grandchildren, and two great-great grandchildren that she is devoted to. Most of her surviving siblings also live in the area. She is in relatively good health. Even a diagnosis of breast cancer during the past year—now in remission—has not slowed her down. Perhaps her parents were right after all, "Whatever God gives you, you take."

Notes

1. Barack Obama, campaign address, Philadelphia, PA, March 18, 2008.
2. Interview, June 9, 2008, South San Francisco, CA.

3. Hildo Pomicpic *A Glimpse of my Life* in Luna M. Jamero ed. *Talk Story: Anthology of Stories by Filipino Americans of the Central Valley of California* Filipino American National Historical Society, Central Valley Chapter (Merced, CA: Carpenter Printing, 2008) and from interview dated September 24, 2008.
4. Manuscript dated November 3, 2008 and various contacts.
5. Interview, June 10, 2008, Richmond, CA.

Bibliography

Agoncillo, Teodoro A. *A Short History of the Philippines* (New York and Toronto: The New American Library, 1969).
Brokaw, Tom. *The Greatest Generation* (New York: Random House, 1998).
Buell, Evangeline Canonizado. *Twenty-Five Chickens and a Pig for a Bride: Growing Up in a Filipino Immigrant Family* (San Francisco: T'Boli Publishing Co., 2006).
Cabezas, Amado, Larry H. Shimagawa, and Gary Kawaguichi. "New Inquiries Into the Socioeconomic Status of Pilipino Americans in California" *Amerasia Journal* 13:1 (1986–87).
Cabreana, Ernie. "Hot Rodding to the Sabong" in *Stories, Legends, and Memories* (Santa Maria: Filipino American National Historical Society, Central Coast Chapter 2008).
Calibjo, Veronica Roslinda. "Biography" in *Stories, Legends, and Memories* (Santa Maria: Filipino American National Historical Society, Central Coast Chapter 2008).
Cordova, Fred. *Filipinos: Forgotten Asian Americans, A Pictorial Essay/1763–circa 1963* (Dubuque IA: Kendall/Hunt Publishing 1983).
Espana-Maram, Linda. *Creating Masculinity in Los Angeles's Little Manila* (New York: Columbia University Press, 2006).
Espiritu, Yen Le. *Filipino American Lives* (Philadelphia: Temple University Press, 1995).
———. "The Intersection of Race, Ethnicity and Class: Multiple Identities of Second-generation Filipinos" *Identities* Vol. 1, No. 2–3 (Overseas Publishers Association 1995).
Herbert, Annalissa Arangcon. *Growing Up Brown in America: The Filipino-Mango Athletic Club of San Francisco 1938–1955* (Unpublished thesis, University of California, Los Angeles, 1996).
Hong, Maxine. *Growing Up Asian American* (New York: Avon Books, 1993).
Jamero, Peter. *Growing Up Brown: Memoirs of a Filipino American* (Seattle: University of Washington Press, 2006).
———. *The Filipino American Young Turks of Seattle: A Unique Experience in the American Sociopolitical Mainstream* in Maria P.P. Root ed. *Filipino Americans: Transformation and Identity* (Thousand Oaks, CA: Sage Publications, 1997).
Kerkvliet, Melinda Tria. *Pablo Manlapit's Fight For Justice* in Jonathan Y. Okamura, Amefil R. Agbayani, and Melinda Tria Kerkvliet guest eds. *Social Process in Hawaii* (University of Hawaii at Manoa, 1991).
Lott, Juanita Tamayo. *Common Destiny: Filipino American Generations* (Lanham, MD: Bowman & Littlefield Publishers, Inc. 2006).
Mannheim, Karl. "Sociology of Generations" *Essays on the Sociology of Culture* (Routledge & Paul Press, 1956).
McReynolds, Patricia Justiniani. *Almost Americans: A Quest For Dignity* (Santa Fe: Red Crane Books, 1997).
Morales, Royal F. *Makibaka, the Pilipino American Struggle* (Los Angeles: Mountainview Publishers, 1974).
Penaranda, Oscar, Serafin Syquia, and Sam Tagactac. "An Introduction to Filipino American Literature," in Frank Chin, et.al. eds. *Aiiieeee! An Anthology of Asian American Writers* (Boston: Harvard University Press, 1974).
Pomicpic, Hildo "A Glimpse of my Life" in Luna M. Jamero ed. *Talk Story: Anthology of Stories by Filipino Americans of the Central Valley of California* Filipino

American National Historical Society, Central Valley Chapter (Merced, CA: Carpenter Printing, 2008).

Posadas, Barbara. "Mestiza Girlhood: Interracial Families in Chicago's Filipino American Community" in *Making Waves: An Anthology of Writings by and about Asian American Women* (Boston: Beacon Press, 1989).

Raymundo, Rizaline R. *Tomorrow's Memories: A Diary, 1924–1928* (Honolulu: University of Hawaii Press, 2003).

Revilla, Linda A. "Filipino American Identity: Transcending the Crisis" in Maria P.P. Root ed. *Filipino Americans: Transformation and Identity* (Thousand Oaks, CA: Sage Publications, 1997).

Santos, Bob. *Hum Bows, Not Hot Dogs: Memoirs of a Savvy Asian American Activist* (Seattle: International Examiner Press, 2002).

Scharlin, Craig and Lilia V. Villanueva. *Philip Vera Cruz: A Personal History of Filipino Immigrants and the Farmworkers Movement* (Seattle: University of Washington Press, 2000).

Sorro, Bill. "A Pickle for the Sun" in Helen Toribio ed. *Seven Card Stud with Seven Manangs Wild: An Anthology of Filipino American Writings* (San Francisco: T'Boli Publishing, 2002).

Takaki, Ronald. *Strangers From a Different Shore: A History of Asian Americans* (New York: Penguin Books, 1989).

U.S. Department of Health, Education, and Welfare in Juanita Tamayo Lott "Demographic Changes Transforming the Filipino American Community" in Maria P.P. Root ed. *Filipino Americans: Transformation and Identity* (Thousand Oaks, CA: Sage Publications, 1997).

Zulueta, Benjamin C. *Book Review of Growing Up Brown* (H-Net Reviews of the Humanities and Social Sciences, December 2007).

Index

Abastillas, Minisio, 106
Aguinid, Alex, 8, 30, 93
Aguinid, Wilma Bucariza, vii, 90–93
Alayu, Frances Belle, 77
Alayu, Francisco Paco, 77
Alayu, Merchora Gadduang, 77
Alayu, Terry , 77
Alayu. Ethel, 77
Andam, Filemon, 87–88
Anderson, Loni, 85
Anolin, Ron, 47
Apilado, Myron, 35
Armada, Karen, iii
Arro, Bobby, 59, 84
Arro, Eugenio Evangelista, 58, 83
Arro, Gloria, 59
Arro, Phil, 83–85
Atentico, Al, 28
Aunt Jemima, 84

Bala, Ernie, 21
Balantac, Deanna, 36
Balcena, Bobby, 36
Baltazar, Gabe, 33
Bambo, Gregorio Bautista, 63
Bambo, Gregory Bautista, vii, 68–71
Banios, Temotea, 58
Basconcillo, Fred, 7, 26, 38, 47
Begonia, Dan, 52
Bobadilla, Pacita Todtod, 34
Boiser, Gabina Hipolito, vii, 104–106
Boiser, Leoncio, 106
Brubeck, Dave, 32
Bucariza, Joseph, 90
Bucariza, Venancio Labrado, 90
Bucariza, William, 90
Buell, Evangeline Canonizado, 2, 33
Bueno, Albert "Corky", 23
Bunac, Felix, 14
Burila, Hamilton, 50

Cabanero, Demitria, 90
Cabreana, Ernie, 12
Cabreana, Gilbertine, 50
Calibjo, Veronica Escalinda, 9, 12

Calegos, Julian, ii, 23, 86
Calica, Nena Tevas, 50
Calica, Rudy, 25, 50
Campos, Dixon, 17, 21, 25, 37, 49, 65
Campos, Ed, 21, 65
Campos, Elisa, 17
Campos, George, 50
Canete, Rufo, 46
Canion, Josie, 50
Canonizado, Evangeline, 8
Cantil, Mary, 9
Cantil, Tani, 52
Carido, Leo, 23
Caruso, 78
Castilliano, Mike, 43, 44
Catiel, Felisa Saavedra, 55
Cayetano, Ben, 37, 51
Chavez, Cesar, 46
Chavez, Eddie, 80
Cobalis, Vince, 21, 37
Concepcion, Cindy, 60
Concepcion, Danny, 60
Concepcion, David, 60
Concepcion, Mercedes Arro, 3, 58, 60
Concepcion, Michael, 60
Concepcion, Ron, 60
Cordero, Jeanne Garcia, 55
Cordova, Dorothy, 39, 43, 44
Cordova, Fred, 1, 3, 29, 39, 43, 44, 50, 52
Cubillo, Henry, 21
Cullinane, Michael, 52

Dacuyan, Henry, 25, 35
Dacuyan, Trongkilino "Chunky", 23
Dagampat, Dick, 36
Daly, William, 47
Dangaran, Ron, 35
Daquioag, Beverley, 50
Davis, Miles, 32
De Vega, Jose, 34
Delphino, Rudy, 7, 25
Diangson, Ticiang, 38
Diangson, William, 37
Docusen, Bernard, 36

Draves, Vicky Manalo, 16, 36
Duag, Felix, 14, 16, 21, 25, 35, 65
Dublin, Albert, 105
Dufresne, Marie, 68
Duldulao, Florence, 48

Enselan, Ernie, 21
Escalante, Leo, 23
Espineda, Simeon, 75
Espiritue, Ye Len, 3, 18
Evangelista, Pedro, 59–60

Fabros, Alex, 52
Fidel, Jose, 36
Flor, Bob, 43, 44
Flores, Larry, 43, 44, 45
Flores, Roy, 43, 44, 45
Fontanilla, James, 38

Gabriel, Roman, 36
Galanida, Dave, 25
Galanida, Emma, 14
Galanida, Jimmy, 25
Galvez, Pete, 23
Garcia, Aurilie, 57–58
Garcia, Henry Demetria, 55
Garcia, Jim, 57, 81
Garcia, Samuel Catiel, vii, 3, 55–58, 81
Garcia, Virginia, 23
Gemoya, "Big Boy", 25
Gemoya, Mo, 25
Gemoya, Pat, 25
Gemoya, Tony, 25
Gillespie, Dizzy, 32
Gin, Chris, 13
Gonzales, Ben, 73
Gonzalez, Dan, 52
Gonzalez, Nina Dublin, vii, 16, 71–75
Gonzalez Jr., Samuel Cecil, vii, 71–75
Gonzalez Sr., Samuel Cecil, 72
Gorre, Sonja, 50
Gorre, Victor, 50
Guingona, Mike, 52

Hara, Sumi (nee Mildred Sevilla), 39
Herbert, Annalissa, 3, 21
Hernandez, Juanita, 86
Hipolito, Ben, 105
Hipolito, Francesca, 104
Hipolito, Frank, 105
Hipolito, Gabina, 10

Hipolito, Leoncio, 104
Hipolito, Sussano, 104–105

Ilumin, Ed, 45
Ilumin, Robert, 45
Itliong, Larry, 46

Jamero, Herb, 23
Jamero, Peter, 43, 51
Jamero, Terri, iii, 43, 44
Jamero-Hada, Julie, iii

Kennedy, John F., 3
Kennedy, Robert F., 3
Kim (nee Villarruz), Primo, 34, 50
King, Martin Luther, 3

Ladaga, Dolores, 9
Lapez, Constancio, 25
Leong, Georgiana, 50, 51
Loable, Jane, 8
Loable, Richard, 10
Los Banos, Domingo, 17, 35
Lott, Juanita Tamayo, 2, 41

MacArthur, General Douglas, 17
Maghoney, Tim, 14
Maglinte, John, 13
Majarucon, Sonny, 23, 34
Malapit, Edwardo, 37
Mama Polonia, 106
Mangaoang, Ernie, 46
Manlapit, Pablo, 46, 102
Mannheim, Kurt, 3, 18
Mansalves, Chris, 46
Marcelo, Ben, 21
McIntyre, Harvey, 43
McReynolds, Patricia Justiniani, 2, 16
Meadowlark Lemon, 87
Megino, Liz, 16
Mendoza, Al, 43, 44
Moncado, Hilario, 2
Monrayo, Angeles, 100–101
Montano, Mike, 34
Morales, Royal, 36, 43, 44
Mullen, James, 22
Munar, Ted, 52
Murray, Bob, 13

Nambatac, Juanita, 14
Navarres, Proceco "Sesong", 22

Niduaza, Otto, 13
Nunez, Joseph "Flip", 34, 50

Obama, Barack, 54
Ochoa, Gloria Megino, 52
Ogilvie, Tony, 43, 44, 45
Olarte, Janet, 98
Olimpio, Emilio, 83
Olimpio, Encarnacion, 83
Olimpio, Julia, vii, 83–86
Organo, Cheryl, iii
Oriarte, Burt, 80–81, 83
Oriarte, George, 23, 80
Oriarte, Jose Valentino, vii, 82–83

Padin, Frank, 22–23
Panoncialman, Jose, 75
Parker, Charlie, 32
Pasquil, Connie, 50
Pasquil, Cornelio, vii, 50, 61–64
Pasquil, Mona, 51
Pasquil, Simenona Rojas, 61
Paular, Josephine Saito Espineda, vii, 52, 75–77
Paular, Ray, vii, 82, 95–98
Plaza, George, 10
Pomicpic, Fred, 25, 87
Pomicpic Jr., Hildo "Sonny", vii, 14, 25, 86–89
Pomicpic Sr., Hildo, 86
Pons, Lily, 78
Posadas, Barbara, 13, 35
Pratt, Elizabeth, 65
Punzal, Cris, 21

Quidichay, Ron, 45

Ramos, Abba, 47
Randall, John, 95
Randall, Virginia Garcia, vii, 25, 94–95
Raymundo, Alejandro Salvador, 101
Raymundo, Donald, 100
Raymundo, Rizaline, vii, 8, 95–104
Revilla, Linda, 3, 15
Reyes, Ted, 50
Robles, Hansel, 60
Romero, Eddie, 16
Romero, Esther Navarro, 103
Romero, Jane, 10
Romero, Terri, 8, 49

Root, Maria, 14
Rosal, Terry, 8

Sabrido, Larry, 21
Saito, Tsuru, 75
Salaver, Patrick, 45
Samson, Frank "Babe", 21, 25, 47
San Buenaventura, Steffi, 52
San Felipe, Clemente, 64
San Felipe, Clemente Joseph, vii, 15, 17, 21, 25, 51, 64–68
San Jose, Bob, 98–99
San Jose, Janet, 99
San Jose Sr., Robert, 98
Santos, Benjamin, 38
Santos, Bob, 2, 12, 13, 36, 43, 44, 52
Sellers, Ruth, 68
Serrano, Pete, 23
Sibonga, Dolores, 37, 43, 44, 52
Soria, Alex, 45
Sorro, Bill, 8
Sugitan, Art, 25, 38
Supat, Richard, 13
Suyat, Stan, 52

Taballeja, Ted, 21, 23
Tangalin, Andres "Sonny", 8, 35, 43, 44
Tecson, Rosie, 50
Tenio Family, 34, 50
Terano, Connie, 7, 16
Tiffany, Dale, 43, 44

Urbiztondo, Adele, 50

Valderama, Abe, 23
Velasco, Pete, 46
Ventura, Ed, 50
Vera Cruz, Philip, 46
Viernes, Connie, 63
Villanueva, Cepy, 21
Villarruz, Primo, 73

Washington, Harold, 79
Whitebear, Bernie, 13
Wightman, Isabel, 72
Wilensky, Michael Diane, 64, 67
Womack, Fran Alayu, vii, 77–80

About The Author

Peter Jamero—a retired health and human services executive now living in Atwater, CA—is the author of *Growing Up Brown: Memoirs of a Filipino American*; *Maeda's Place*; and *The Filipino Young Turks of Seattle: A Unique Experience in the American Sociopolitical Mainstream.* He was formerly director of the Washington State Division of Vocational Rehabilitation; director of the King County (WA) Department of Human Resources; vice president of the United Way of King County; executive director of the San Francisco Human Rights Commission; assistant professor of Rehabilitation Medicine of the University of Washington; branch chief in the U.S. Department of Health, Education, and Welfare in Washington, D.C.; and executive director of the Asian American Recovery Services in San Francisco.